Golf Courses and Resorts around the World

GOLF
COURSES AND RESORTS AROUND THE WORLD

A comprehensive guide to the world's best luxury
golf destinations including a mix of history, course
architecture and tips on how to play each course

DANIEL FALLON

NEW
HOLLAND

Contents

The Chateau Elan & The Vintage, New South Wales, Australia .

Introduction

Southern Cape Owner's Club, Gyeongsangnam-do, South Korea.

Standing on the crow's nest-like tee of 'Widow's Walk' at Cape Kidnappers, it feels like I'm having an out-of-body experience. My giddiness might have something to do with the nearby cliff's edge. It's a vertical drop of hundreds of feet to the Pacific Ocean. Close by, I watch a gannet glide towards me on the southerly. White cliffs stand in contrast to the emerald waters below.

The sheer beauty of this scene near Napier in New Zealand's North Island is something I'll never forget – even if my poor drive off the tee was something I'd like to. Here, renowned American golf architect Tom Doak has created a challenging links-style course using the natural contours of the land. The fairways sit between deep ravines and look like long green fingers from the air, extending to the edge of these magnificent cliffs above the Pacific on the back nine. While the golf was unforgettable, dinner back at The Farm – our luxury accommodation, which sits on 6,000 acres (2,428 hectares) of farmland – was simply sublime. Five courses of the most delicious, succulent food made from local fare, each matched with wine from the nearby Hawke's Bay vineyards. In combination with the luxurious boutique accommodation, a heated infinity pool and jacuzzi that looked over the bay itself, and spa treatments to pamper the love of my life, this is a getaway that we still talk about. (The fact that the resort helped organize a day of rafting on a wild New Zealand river – one of my wife's favorite outdoors activities – also helped.)

And this wonderful golfing trip got me thinking. What if I created a bucket list of dream golfing destinations around the world and set out to play them? Golf resorts that are set in some of the globe's most stunning locations that feature courses which are challenging and exhilarating to play for both a keen amateur, such as myself, and the scratch golfer alike. Resorts that offer brilliant accommodation, exceptional service, and world-class dining. But they would also need to offer other activities to enthrall a partner who was not necessarily a golfer – whether it be Pilates classes, a rejuvenating massage or a horse-riding adventure.

And, essentially, that is what I have attempted to achieve here with the guidance of my New Holland commissioning editor Alan Whiticker. Thanks to regular golf travel writing for *The Sydney Morning Herald* and *The Age* newspapers over a period of 17 years, I have been privileged indeed to visit many world-class golf resorts. My travels have taken me through New Zealand, the United States, parts of Asia and my home country of Australia. Whether it was driving a ball through thin air at the Royal Nepal Golf Course in Kathmandu, or weaving a seven-iron between lava flows on Hualalai on the island of Hawaii, I have enjoyed some extraordinary rounds of golf.

I have been lucky enough to stay as a guest in some extraordinary properties set in the world's most beautiful locations, such as at Aspen's five-star, five-diamond hotel The Little Nell, which turns from luxury ski lodge in winter to summer activities hub with high-altitude golf at Aspen Golf Club, cycling adventures and guided fly-fishing expeditions. From this, all the way to taking an unforgettable helicopter tour of the stunning mountains that surround Queenstown between rounds whilst

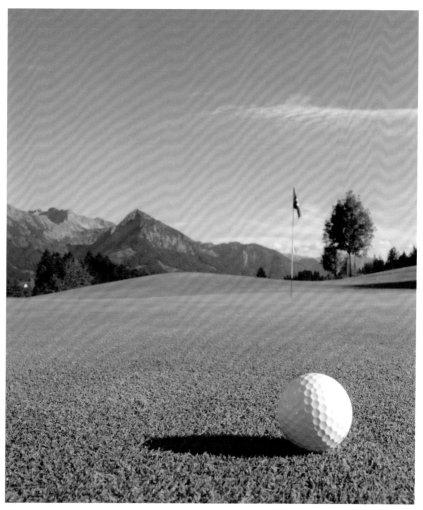

Oberallgäu, Germany.

staying at the Rees Hotel on Lake Wakatipu in New Zealand. Memories are forged both on and off fairways.

But this is just a start – my experience is relatively limited compared to many golf writers in other parts of the world. To do this list of dream golf destinations thoroughly, and decide who would make the top 50, I needed the help of golf experts from all over the globe. Experts such as Robert Fagan, who has played over 3,000 courses, stayed at over 1,000 golf resorts and is one of North America's most travelled and respected golf writers. Then there is the thriving world of Asian golf, witnessed best by Japan's Masa Nishijima, a course design consultant and the author of the award-winning book, *Analysis of a Golf Course.*

European golf writer Jo Maes and German golf journalist Ulrich Mayring were instrumental in covering European resorts. *Golf Digest South Africa* editor Stuart McLean tipped me off to the brilliant golf holidays offered in Mauritius as well as South Africa, while Canadian golf writer Dave Finn became a key assistant and sounding board. (See page 329, to meet my experts).

Selecting the world's top golf resorts is an inexact science; I have not visited each one in person. But I'm confident in the thoroughness of the method I've used to select each golf destination on the wish list. There are many great golf resorts that have not been included due to space limitations.

I've gone to great lengths to consider as many leading golf resorts as possible through my own research and by canvassing well-regarded golf writers, course designers and professional players about what they consider to be the top golf resorts and why. By gathering this expert panel and being guided by their experiences and knowledge, I believe I have established a list of truly remarkable golf destinations. They are presented here in alphabetical order.

These resorts offer different vacation experiences – for some, the challenges and quality of the golf course rises above all features, such as that of Tasmania's Barnbougle Dunes /Lost Farm. Others, such as Teluk Datai on the tropical island of Langkawi, offer a romantic escape for couples and extraordinary jungle golf. Still others have enough features to satisfy the entire family – such as Turtle Bay Resort on the Hawaiian Island of Oʻahu (send the kids on a surf lesson). All of them are stay-and-play destinations – the accommodation has a close association with the golf course. There are some brilliant golf courses that don't fit these criteria that have been left out, such as the acclaimed Royal County Down and neighboring Slieve Donard Hotel in Northern Island, but I'll gladly play them too if I get the chance.

As a guide to playing each course, I've tried to get tips from the professionals at each resort as well as a comment from the course architect where possible. I've included information on the slope rating (how hard a course is for amateur golfers – the higher the harder), course rating (or standard scratch score – what a scratch golfer should score), as well as yardage from the championship tees to help indicate how hard the course will play. Never fear, the courses have forward tees to suit different standards of golfers.

When I tell people about writing *Golf Courses and Resorts around the World*, the reaction is often similar. For those who love golf, a dreamy look overtakes their features as they imagine the possibilities. For a moment, they are teeing off at Pebble Beach or some other iconic location. Many of them have enjoyed golf vacations and they know how memorable they can be. Those who are not golfers even concede the project sounds like fun, especially when it involves fine food or a daiquiri by the pool.

And on that note, I hope you raise a glass now and enjoy dreaming a little with me about your next golf vacation, for here are the *Golf Courses and Resorts around the World*.

Pacific Dunes, Hole No.10, Bandon Dunes, Oregon, United States.

THE RESORTS

The Abaco Club
at Winding Bay

The Abaco Club at Winding Bay

Location: Cherokee Road on Winding Bay, Marsh Harbour, Abaco, The Bahamas
Website: theabacoclub.com
Phone number: 242 367 0077

The Bahamas is synonymous with tropical beaches, warm turquoise water, and vacations in the sun – and the perfect spot for golf. You'll find all this at the Abaco Club at Winding Bay, which is located on the east side of Great Abaco, one of the largest islands in the coral-based archipelago that makes up the Commonwealth of the Bahamas. The resort is approximately 193 miles (310 kilometres) east of Miami or about one hour's flight to Marsh Harbour International Airport.

Golfers are drawn to the championship course here – a Scottish-style links course that overlooks a white, powder-soft beach on one side and the North Atlantic Ocean on the other side. Renowned British architects Tom Mackenzie and Donald Steel designed the course over coastal dunes, including pot bunkers and slick, undulating greens. You may have to snap out of your tropical island slumber to score well here. The Abaco Club hosted the Bahamas Great Abaco Classic, a Web.com Tour event, in 2017, (and it will return in 2018). So you may want to warm up on the practice range and short-game practice area before teeing off.

'It is not the typical, short Caribbean holiday course of the sort affiliated with most Caribbean resorts,' warned Head Professional Robert Blumer. 'It requires thought, imagination, patience and skill to score well here.

'The course looks – and plays – like a links golf course, which is the ideal configuration for an island course where wind is almost always a factor. The pot bunkers, the swales in the fairways, the vexing greens, the hard-and-true nature of both the fairways and greens – these all provide a links golf experience, but in the warm Bahamian sunshine rather than the cold rain of the British Isles.'

The idea of heading back to the resort pool after a tough round here is appealing. But first you'll be hitting along the shore of Winding Bay's tranquil turquoise waters on the front nine, before the back nine plays along the cliff-top shoreline with the swell from the Atlantic crashing down next to you. It attracts some of the top players in the game, too, according to Blumer. 'Top touring professionals Darren Clarke and Thomas Aiken are both club members and residents of the club, both love playing the course (Clarke prepares every year for The Masters here), and the new practice facility with double-sided range and extensive short-game practice area help them stay at the top of their games.'

OPPOSITE: The Abaco Club Course.

The challenges

Keep your ball out of the pot bunkers. You may need to lower your trajectory if the wind gets up, too. The elevated greens require accurate and pure pitch and chip shots. Pro's tips: 'The key to scoring well at The Abaco Club is placing your approach shots on the right part of the greens – or if you do miss a green, not short-siding yourself. The greens generally have three or more contoured sections – finding the right one with your approach makes two-putting much easier.'

The resort experience

The Abaco Club on Winding Bay is a private sporting club for homeowners and members that opens its doors to visitors staying at the resort. English entrepreneur and sailor Peter de Savary founded the club in 2004. The story goes that he sailed

Type of grasses: The greens and fairways are Paspalum, a salt-water resistant grass that flourishes in the Bahamian sunshine. Zoysia grass was used in the areas surrounding the course's white-sand bunkers.

When to play: Perfect golfing temperatures allow the course to be open 365 days a year.

Par: 72

Yardage: 7,111 yards, 6,502 metres

Slope: 136

Rating: 75.1

Best hole: The 312-yard (285-metre) hole 5 is a driveable par 4, but you must carry your tee shot over a beach. Miss the green and you could be playing from the beach or from a pot bunker. Lay-up and you must judge the wedge shot well onto a green that slopes sharply from right to left. There are some spectacular views of Winding Bay along the left side.

The general manager says: 'One of the most scenic courses anyone will ever play... The course is a true championship course, as shown during play at the Bahamas Great Abaco Classic, a Web.com event featuring some of the world's best golfers. What sets it apart from other courses, and particularly from other Caribbean golf courses, is that it is a bona fide links design.' – Robert Blumer, Abaco Club Head Professional into the bay, hacked through the jungle for a spell with a machete and was mightily impressed by the location, which has two miles (three kilometres) of beach on the south side, and tall cliffs on the east side. Savary then spent a fortune building the luxury resort and golf course, opening the resort for members who wanted to get away from it all. This is the type of place where you'd expect that the bartender knows the drinks of the regulars, most of them rich and some of them famous. Celebrities such as Annika Sorenstam and Rod Stewart have been known to visit. Club ambassador and Europe's 2016 Ryder Cup Captain Darren Clarke loves the low-key nature of the resort.

'I love the relaxed atmosphere here,' Clarke said*. 'It's extraordinarily beautiful, and there's no place I'd rather spend time, especially with my family.

'One of the things that I particularly like about The Abaco Club is the fact that, strictly speaking, it's not a resort. Anyone can visit the Club (and I highly recommend that you do!) but in truth, it's a private, international sporting club with members from all over the world.'

The resort's infinity pool looks out onto Winding Bay, over the nearby Sugar Cay and out to sea. It's not a bad spot for a cocktail. The full-service spa offers healing massages such as the Bahamian Rhythmic Touch Therapy. You can also employ a personal trainer in the fitness centre to burn some extra calories.

The Abaco Club is about 25 minutes' drive south of Marsh Harbour International Airport.

Dine and wine

There are three options for catered dining. Flippers Beach Bar serves fresh Bahamian fruit for breakfast as well as lunch in a part tiki hut, part café. Wednesday is barbecue night with live music, a bonfire on the beach and 's'mores' for the children. The Cliff House overlooks Winding Bay from a ridge at Ocean Point. It specializes in fresh, locally-caught seafood, including grouper and lobster. You can also book a chef to come and cook at your rental home's kitchen.

The accommodation

The difference at this resort is that instead of a regular hotel, you'll be renting a vacation property. You can opt for a one-bedroom Cabana (570 square feet, 53 square metres), two- three- or four-bedroom Cottage or an Estate Home. The Cabana sleeps two in a compact dwelling that features modern furniture, a screened-in porch, high ceilings and air conditioning. It's a short walk to the beach through the lush tropical bush. The 2–4 bedroom Cottages have an open-planned kitchen, chic furniture, bathroom with tub and dual vanities, and living room area.

Other activities

The resort attracts deep-sea and salt-water fly-fishermen. A boat ride of about 15 minutes will get you to the edge of the reef and a deep drop-off that is good for targeting tuna, mahi, marlin, grouper and other trophy fish. Alternatively, salt-water fly-fishing on the flats is world-class, too. Darren Clarke landed a 38-pound permit, just short of the world record, near the club. Some water sports equipment is provided free for guests. Snorkel off the beach to Sugar Cay and try to spot a sea turtle or large tropical fish. And take out a paddleboard or Hobie Cat. The Sea of Abaco is sheltered by shoals and cays, making it a good area for sailing and boating as well. Scuba diving can also be organized to explore coral dive sites. The club's concierge can help organize your adventures. Tennis courts are also available.

*Source: theabacoclub.com

OPPOSITE: Abaco Club Cliff Cottage Pool; *ABOVE:* Abaco Club Cliff House Deck Bar.

The American Club

Wisconsin, United States

The American Club

Location: N8501 Lakeshore Road, Sheboygan, Wisconsin, 53083, United States
Website: www.americanclubresort.com/golf/whistling-straits
Phone number: 1855 444 2838

About an hour's drive north from Milwaukee, the American Club can be found in the small Wisconsin town of Kohler next to the Sheboygan River and the city of Sheboygan. What started as a house built in 1918 for immigrant workers who came to work for Walter J. Kohler's Kohler Company (think kitchen and bathroom products) has eventually transformed into one of the best golf resorts in the world.

Kohler wanted to provide board for foreigners and a positive social setting for them to assimilate into American society. He said at the opening on June 23; 1918: 'The name, American Club, was decided upon as it was thought that, with high standards of living and clean healthful recreation, it would be a factor in inculcating in men of foreign antecedents a love for their adopted country.'*

The American Club opened as a luxury hotel in 1981 and now offers four championship courses for visitors divided between two facilities: Blackwolf Run opened in 1988, featuring The River and The Meadow Valleys courses next to the Sheboygan River; and Whistling Straits, which first welcomed golfers in 1998 to the Straits Course next to Lake Michigan, and then The Irish, a links-style course, in 2000 just inland of it. Whistling Straits is about 15 minutes' drive from the American Club.

The Straits is famous for hosting the PGA Championship in 2004, 2010 and 2015, won by Vijay Singh, Martin Kaymer and Jason Day respectively. It was also the site of the US Senior Open in 2007, which was won by Brad Bryant, and is set to be the battleground for the 2020 Ryder Cup. It is an imposing links-style course in terms of distance at 7,790 yards (7,123 metres) as well as having over 1,000 bunkers, according to Mike O'Reilly, Head Golf Professional at Whistling Straits. It can be a frightening view from the tee block, but the landing zone is in view and it is more playable than your first impression might suggest, he said.

'There are 1,000 bunkers but not every one of them is going to come into play. You could be looking off in the distance and see a series of eight bunkers that are 200 yards off the fairway. They are not going to come into play, but as you are looking at the hole, it's part of your view so it's kind of visually intimidating for the player.

'As you are looking at its different holes, you're in awe of what you see but then, after you play the hole … (you find) it is very playable.'

The Straits Course, a walking-only layout, was designed to look and play like a classic links course in Ireland or Scotland. Eight holes hug the shoreline of Lake

Michigan and there are a lot of mounds and dunes throughout the layout as the course rolls with the undulations of the land.

The Irish Course is similar in style to the Straits with its bunkering and dunes but doesn't have the aesthetic beauty of being lakeside. There are four streams that wind across the layout and 10 wooden bridges to cross them. Nearly 2,000 trees were planted in the creation of this course.

Blackwolf Run is a few minutes' drive from the American Club. The facility is named after Chief Black Wolf, who led a Winnebago Indian tribe in the region some 200 years ago.

The River Course has the Sheboygan River running through it and is, according to O'Reilly, 'One of the most beautiful American-style golf courses that you'll find

Type of grasses: The Irish, Meadow Valleys and River courses have bentgrass on tees, fairways and greens. The Straits Course has tees and greens of bentgrass but the fairways are fescue, which is thinner and stands up taller, like classic links courses in the UK.

When to play: The courses typically open on April 10 and the season runs until November 15. Although the peak is in June, the fall colors later in the season are stunning. This is one brutally cold place between December and March.

Par: All four golf courses are par 72.

Slope / Rating / Yardage: Blackwolf Run Meadow Valley: 145 / 75.1 / 7,250 yards, 6,629 metres River Course: 151 / 76.2 / 7,404 yards,

6,770 metres Whistling Straits The Straits: 152 / 77.2 / 7,790 yards, 7,123 metres Irish Course: 146 / 75.6 / 7,201 yards, 6,585 metres

The pro says: 'As a resort, what is really unique here is that we have four golf courses and they are all four unique experiences. They are challenging courses. I'd say of the four, the Meadow Valleys and The Irish are probably the tamest and they are rated that way as well. The River Course is very much a target golf course – if you miss-hit the fairway you are going to pay a severe penalty – and the Straits Course is long. If it is windy – it is right on the shore of a huge lake and we can get a lot of wind here – it can get very challenging.' – Mike O'Reilly, Head Golf Professional Whistling Straits anywhere'. The river comes into play on 14 holes and the course also has challenging bunkering and large undulating greens. This 7,404-yard (6,770-metre) layout requires strategic hitting and excellent ball control.

'The River Course is very much a target golf course – if you miss-hit the fairway you are going to pay a severe penalty,' O'Reilly said. The Meadow Valleys Course is the easiest of the four courses and a tale of two nines, with a flatter opening followed by an outstanding closing run that is built into a valley and features a lot of undulations. 'If you ask any of the staff members here 'what is the best nine at the resort?', they are going to say the back nine at Meadow Valleys.'

Golf Digest ranked the Straits Course No. 51 in its list of *The World's 100 Greatest Courses 2016–17* and the River Course No. 16 in its list of *America's 100 Greatest Public Courses.*

The challenges

On the Straits Course, the huge distance from the back tees (7,790 yards, 7,123 metres) and enormous number of bunkers (over 1,000) will be tough to overcome. Along with the undulating fairways and large, slick greens, it is no wonder the course rating is 77.2. The Irish Course has similar challenges with bunkering as well as four

PREVIOUS PAGE: Whistling Straits. *ABOVE:* Golf course view.

streams to contend with, but those pale in comparison to the River Course, which has 14 holes with water in play and requires you to stay on the fairway and hit your targets. The natural undulations of the Meadow Valleys course on the back nine will intrigue players but this is the easiest course.

The accommodation:
The American Club is a five-star, five-diamond hotel that has a lot to offer guests in each season of the year. The redbrick building was once an immigrant dormitory and pub in the early 20th Century, but now offers accommodation and services at the height of luxury. The rooms feature opulent and modern interiors and décor. Next door to this historic hotel is the five-star Kohler Waters Spa, which offers a variety of water-inspired treatments such as hydrotherapy as well as massage treatments. There's even a rooftop deck with a lounge, fireplace and jacuzzi. The American Club was listed as one of the *Top 15 Wellness Retreats in the World* by *Conde Nast Traveler* in 2017, as well as receiving *Golf Magazine's* Platinum Award for Premier Resorts – 2016–17.

Other Kohler accommodation can be found at the three-diamond Inn on Woodlake (121 boutique-style guest rooms by a scenic lake) and Sandhill cabin, a secluded retreat on 350 acres (142 hectares) of Wisconsin wilderness. Both of these options give you access to the resort facilities. Most of the resort's outdoor activities can be found at River Wildlife Lodge, which is about a mile (two kilometres) away. A shuttle service can transport you to the various Kohler facilities and properties.

Dine and wine

The American Club features four restaurants and one bar. Enjoy four-star, four-diamond dining at The Immigrant Room, which actually has six rooms dedicated to early Wisconsin settlers from Germany, France, Denmark, The Netherlands, England and Normandy. The contemporary American cuisine has European influences. I'll be starting with a King Crab, progressing to the 30-Day Aged Prime Tenderloin with Béarnaise sauce and finishing with the Vanilla Crème Brûlée. A Californian Cabernet Sauvignon will go well nicely with it. Otherwise you have the Horse & Plow tavern (pub fare), Wisconsin Room (the original dining hall for immigrants with locally-sourced, seasonal food), The Green House (pastries, ice cream and afternoon tea), and the Winery Bar (fine wine with Wisconsin cheeses). River Wildlife Lodge has a restaurant that has Midwestern fare for lunch with a game theme. Inn on Woodlake has one restaurant and three cafes. You'll find fine dining and superb views at the Blackwolf Run and Whistling Straits restaurants, too. And sleepy heads don't have to get out of bed to enjoy fine food with the 24-hour room service, as well.

The accommodation

The plush interiors include fine hand-crafted furniture. The Standard Room (263–349 square feet, 24–32 square metres) has upholstered chairs, ottoman, work table and king-size bed or two doubles. The Presidential Suite (1429 square feet, 133 square metres) has two wet bars, a separate powder room, fireplace, and a King Baker bed. Those on a smaller budget should consider the Inn on Woodlake or secluded Sandhill cabin.

Other activities

There are plenty of activities to enjoy in summer and winter at the American Club. Perhaps starting with some Yoga on the Lake (35 classes a week) by Wood Lake or head to Sports Core Health & Racquet Club for tennis, swimming, the jacuzzi and steam room. Young people can sign up for Kohler Kids with games, crafts and movies at the Inn on Woodlake, but the whole family can enjoy the nature walks (all seasons) and pedal boating, canoeing and kayaking in summer. Snowshoeing, ice skating and sledding are all available in winter. Many of the outdoor adventures take place out of River Wildlife Lodge where you can go on a guided horseback trail ride, try trap, clay, or air-rifle target shooting, and fish for trout and salmon as they make their way up the Sheboygan River in season.

*Source: www.americanclubresort.com

Best hole(s): The Straits Course's intimidating hole No. 17 features a 249-yard (228-metre) par 3 that hugs the shore of Lake Michigan. You'll want to miss the large pot bunker on the right side of the green, while the left side has a 20-foot (6-metre) drop off to a series of bunkers before reaching the water. The Irish Course's 398-yard (364-metre) hole 10 is a beautiful and difficult par-4 dogleg left, with mounds, dunes and bunkers on the right of the fairway and a large green protected by several bunkers and a sharp drop off the back. On the River Course, the 427-yard (390-metre) par-4 hole 5 has an elevated tee that gives you a stunning view of the fairway, green and Sheboygan River. It has a large bunker on the right and small pot bunkers down the left side of the fairway as well as a large undulating green. 'In the fall, when the leaves have changed and the salmon are running up the river, it's hard to find a better hole in the world,' said O'Reilly. And on Meadow Valleys, the 227-yard (208-metre) hole 15 is a par 3 you will remember. You must carry a large valley to a sloping 18,000-square-foot (1,672-square-metre) putting surface.

ABOVE: The Straits course. *OPPOSITE:* Activities at River Wildlife Lodge include trap shooting.

The Langer Course, Ile Aux Cerfs.

Anahita the Resort

Anahita the Resort

Location: Beau Champ, Grande Rivière Sud Est 40901, Mauritius
Website: anahita.mu ; www.fourseasons.com/mauritius/golf ;
www.ileauxcerfsgolfclub.com
Phone number: 230 402 2200

Mauritius is a small island nation that sits a little over 680 miles (1,100 kilometres) to the east of Madagascar. Anahita the Resort is located on the east coast of Mauritius, about one hour's drive from the capital, Port Louis. The resort features two championship courses that overlook the Indian Ocean – one designed by South African Ernie Els and the other designed by German Bernhard Langer. The all-inclusive resort package allows you to play both courses as part of the deal, and includes 55 range balls and a daily one-hour introductory lesson.

Completed in 2008, the Els course is managed by Four Seasons Golf Club Mauritius at Anahita and features wide fairways and great views of the coastline. The 7,467-yard (6,828-metre) layout winds its way through tropical vegetation with a turquoise lagoon on one side and jagged mountain peaks in the backdrop on the other. Six of the holes run next to the shore, including three that provide a scenic finish that carries through to the last green, which is well protected by bunkers. The par-5 18th fairway passes a lagoon on the left, and stone ruins on the right side.

The Ernie Els course hosted the Mauritius Open in 2016, a European-, Sunshine- and Asian-Tour-sanctioned event. It made an impression on 2016 South African Open winner Brandon Stone who competed in the event. 'It's stunning. You stand on that 17th tee box, you just overlook the estuary and you can see the waves crashing on the coral.'*

At the end of the round, the Il Forno Restaurant & Bar is there for some Mediterranean-style food or a cleansing ale. Ernie's Shooter is the recommended drink. The Four Seasons Golf Academy can provide video analysis of your swing if you are looking to work on your technique, best before an Ernie's Shooter.

The Bernhard Langer-designed Ile Aux Cerfs Golf Course (also known as Le Touessrok) is laid out across 94 acres (38 hectares) of a small island just off the coast from the Anahita resort. So, you'll be taking your golf clubs on a boat shuttle that leaves every 30 minutes. Ile Aux Cerfs is a stunning-looking course woven into a lush tropical island setting that was previously the site of an old sugar plantation. Players will hit the ball off undulating fairways that pass volcanic rock outcrops, white-sand beaches, lakes, massive bunkers and gullies. The course was renovated in 2014–15 to make it easier for higher handicappers. From the tips, seven of the holes require carries over 200 yards (183 metres) of water so it will test the nerves.

OPPOSITE: Els Course, Anahita the Resort.

The Ernie Els course was ranked No.3 and Ile Aux Cerfs No.1 in Mauritius by Top100GolfCourses.com in 2017.

The challenges

These are tough courses. The Ernie Els course will challenge you for distance with 7,500 yards (6,828 metres) as you avoid strategically-placed bunkers, while the Bernhard Langer course has nine lakes and seven holes that require you to carry over water with solid strikes. Three of these are over sea inlets.

The resort experience

It's worth watching out for deals at Four Seasons, but Anahita the Resort's all-inclusive package is hard to beat. This luxury resort is spread out over 213 hectares (526 acres) of tropical gardens next to the Il Aux Cerfs Lagoon. It has two beaches – one that looks out on the Indian Ocean and the other by the lagoon – a fitness centre, tennis courts, a water sports centre and a wellness centre. There is a tropical island feel to the design of the suites and villas with thatched roofs a common feature amongst the palm trees. The Anahita Spa by Thémaé Paris has a focus on tea-based treatments and products. It also has a steam room and jacuzzi. The OurSpace Kids' Club and Escape Teens' Club have plenty of activities for the young people. Lounging under an umbrella on a seat on the beach with daiquiri within reach is the right approach to resort golf.

Dine and wine

With five restaurants, a coffee shop and in-suite dining (private chef option and room service), you won't go hungry. Starting at breakfast, you'll find international fare and local dishes at Origine Restaurant, then fine dining with Mauritian specialties at the Signature Restaurant, Italian dishes overlooking Els' 18th hole at Il Forno:

Trattoria Restaurant, Mauritian and Mediterranean fare at Bliss Beach Restaurant and Domaine De L'Etoile Restaurant, which is set in nearby tropical bushland. Back at the resort, The Vu Bar has live bands on weekends and a DJ during the week if you want to dance.

The accommodation
The Prestige Villas come in one- to five-bedroom options. These have modern interiors with comfortable décor, king-size beds, en suite bathrooms, a full kitchen, a living room, LCD TVs and a swimming pool. The Prestige Suites come with one or two bedrooms, a terrace with lagoon views, a living area, kitchen and bathroom with tub and dual vanities, and as an added treat, an infinity plunge pool.

Other activities
Domaine de l' Etoile – a nature reserve that covers over 2,965 acres (1,200 hectares) of forests, pastures, rivers – is only 15 minutes away. Explore the beautiful surrounds on foot, quad bike, horse or buggy. Or stay closer to the resort and get wet. You'll find kayaks, Hobie Cats, windsurfers and paddle boats. You can also take a closer look at the coral on a snorkelling or scuba diving trip or on a glass-bottom boat tour. Kids will love the Adventure Park, which has a zip line and other tree-top activities. The fitness centre has yoga, boxing, core workouts, Pilates and aqua-gym.

*Source: afrasiabankmauritiusopen.com

**Source: www.tcsworldtravel.com/blog/ile-aux-cerfs-mauritius-private-golf-course

ABOVE: Langer Course. *OPPOSITE:* Origine Restaurant.

Type of grasses: Els course has fairways of Bermuda Tif419 and TifDwarf Bermuda turf greens. The Langer course has Salam Seashore Paspalum.

When to play: Year-round – it's a tropical climate with little change in seasons.

Par: Both courses 72

Slope / Rating / Yardage: Els Course 147 / 74 / 7,500 yards, 6,828 metres Langer Course (Ile Aux Cerfs): 155 / 75 / 7,115 yards, 6,469 metres

Best hole: The signature hole on the Els course is No.4. Dubbed 'The Ocean Drive,' you have to avoid fairway bunkers on the left off the tee, before hitting to a green that sits on a peninsular almost surrounded by water, with bunkers placed just behind it. On the Langer course, the 410-yard (375-metre) hole 18 poses a tough test. Called 'Back to the Boat', this par 4 requires you to carry mangroves off the tee before hitting to a three-tiered green.

The pro says: 'The course is consistently well conditioned, with spectacular views, and a selection of tees to suit all levels of golf. The Il Forno restaurant will have something to replenish your energy for another round!' – Dave Usendorff, Director of Golf at the Ernie Els Course

Bandon Dunes, Hole No. 16.

Bandon Dunes

Oregon, United States

Bandon Dunes

Location: 57744 Round Lake Road, Bandon, Oregon, 97411, USA
Website: bandondunesgolf.com
Phone number: 1 888 345 6008; 1 541 347 4380

The story of how arguably the world's top golf resort came to be is a good one. Mike Keiser, an entrepreneur who made his money printing gift cards on recycled paper, fell in love with golf and, in particular, links golf. Instead of just playing top courses at private clubs around the world he felt the need to create his own brilliant layouts, but a key motivating factor was to keep the courses open to the public. It's an everyman sentiment that's sometimes at odds with the exclusive world of privileged golf in America, but one that should be encouraged. His first project was to build a nine-hole course by Lake Michigan – the Dunes Club turned out to be one of the finest layouts in America. Keiser was just getting started.

After spotting a beautiful dune landscape on the Pacific Coast of Oregon, he set out transforming it into a dream destination for golfers. Keiser brought in Scottish architect David McLay Kidd to build links course Bandon Dunes in 1999 (ranked 90 in *The World's 100 Greatest Golf Courses – 2016–17* by *Golf Digest*), and then American Tom Doak to build Pacific Dunes (ranked 39 in the world by *Golf Digest*), which opened in 2001. Both courses have multiple holes that work along the bluffs overlooking the coast. They were celebrated layouts from the start.

'Holes seem to emerge from the landscape rather than being superimposed onto it,' *Golf Digest*'s Ron Whitten wrote of Pacific Dunes. 'The rolling greens and rumpled fairways are framed by rugged sand dunes and marvelously grotesque bunkers.'

Despite already getting the attention of golfers around the world, Keiser kept building courses. Acclaimed US architects Bill Coore and Ben Crenshaw were brought in to design Bandon Trails, which was completed in 2005. The layout starts in the dunes before heading through forest and finally finishing in the dunes. (Coore and Crenshaw returned to build Bandon Preserve, a 13-hole par 3 course in 2012 that ranks well in the US).

The fourth course, Old MacDonald, was designed by Tom Doak and Jim Urbina in 2010 to try to emulate the work of legendary architect C.B. Macdonald at the National Golf Links in Southhampton, New York. *Golf Digest* ranked Old Macdonald No. 47 and Bandon Trails No. 70 in its list of *America's 100 Greatest Courses – 2016–2017*.

How do the Bandon links courses compare? Bandon Dunes, the most mature course, is routed over the bluffs and ends back at the main lodge. Pacific Dunes is the

OPPOSITE: Pacific Dunes Course.

shortest links course here with the smallest greens and natural sand-dune bunkers. Bandon Trails is a links layout cut into a forest setting and it traverses a massive dune that divides the property from east to west. Old Macdonald features some of the largest greens you'll find anywhere.

What sets Bandon Dunes Resort apart from many is that it is a retreat with links golf as the focus – four championship courses – and the resort itself doesn't have any residential housing or major development built onto the land. It is golf played in a beautiful and natural environment. You'll burn some calories too – this is a walking-only golf resort.

The challenges

This is nirvana for those who love links play. The wind whips off the Pacific Ocean to the west, adding to the level of difficulty so you may want to keep the ball trajectory lower, depending on the conditions, as well as employing bump and run tactics near the greens. The pro's tips? 'Learn to use your putter from everywhere around the greens and flight your full swings. The trajectory of your full shots is key with distance control.'

Type of grasses: All the courses have fine fescue fairways and greens with small amounts of bent and poa.

When to play: The courses are open year-round. The average temperature in January is 55° Fahrenheit, or 12.7° Celsius, according to Weather.com. The green fees at Bandon Dunes change with the season but are not overly priced.

Par: Pacific Dunes par 71 Bandon Dunes par 72 Bandon Trails par 71 Old Macdonald par 71

Rating / Slope / Yardage: Bandon Dunes 74.1 / 143 / 6,732 yards, 6,156 metres Pacific Dunes 73 / 142 / 6,633 yards, 6,065 metres Old Macdonald 74.4 / 131 / 6,944 yards, 6,350 metres Bandon Trails 73.6 / 130 / 6,759 yards, 6,180 metres

The pro says: 'All of the courses are authentic links courses that demand every shot imaginable. Their routings are the perfect blend between long demanding holes and short strategic ones.'
– Michael Chupka Jr. PGA

The resort experience

Bandon Dunes is a retreat for keen golfers. The lodge and other buildings are in line with the minimalist approach of the courses. They fit into the environment without being overbearing – grey metals roofs, wooden shingles and plenty of wooden chairs outside to enjoy the view of the golf course, dunes and ocean in the distance. You'll find the massage centre, sauna and jacuzzi are all good spots to ease the muscles after playing a couple of courses here. The resort prides itself on the small-town friendly service it offers guests.

Dine and wine

There are four eateries to choose from. You can enjoy fine dining, including fine wine, at The Gallery in the lodge. Trails End restaurant includes Asian dishes on their menu as well as views overlooking Bandon Trails' Hole 18 (a good spot to watch sunset with cocktail in hand). The Pacific Grill, next to the Punchbowl course, has daily fish specials and some good drinks. Finally, McKee's Pub has hearty fare such as Grandma's Meatloaf, which would go well with a freshly poured Guinness and Grandma for company if you can get her to Oregon.

The accommodation

With five separate accommodation options, you'll find something to fit the budget and group size. The Lily Pond rooms offer the best value. You get two queen-sized beds, a fireplace, sitting area and private deck looking out on the lily pond and forest. Those in a larger group may go with the Lodge Suite, which has four bedrooms, each with a separate bathroom and a balcony overlooking Bandon Dunes and the Pacific Ocean.

ABOVE: The Lodge; OPPOSITE: Bandon Trails Course.

Other activities

If you have time after playing all the courses, head out on the hiking trails that lead to the beach, or enter the on-site labyrinth, which replicates a maze at Chartres Cathedral in France, as well as other loops that work around the property. Fishermen, such as myself, can engage a guide to take them salmon or steelhead trout-fishing when they spawn on their way up local freshwater streams and rivers.

ABOVE: Punchbowl, a 100,000-square-foot putting course; *BELOW:* McKee's Pub.
OPPOSITE ABOVE: Old MacDonald Course; *OPPOSITE BELOW:* Double bedroom.

Best hole: Bandon Dunes, Hole 16. This is a 363-yard (332-metre) par 4 that has a tee shot with the wind over the bluffs to a split fairway. Cliffs that overlook a beach and the Pacific are on your right-hand side as you hit your approach shot.

Pacific Dunes, Hole 13. A 444-yard (406-metre) par 4 made longer as you hit into the prevailing wind onto an undulating fairway.

It'll be a relief to land the ball on the elevated green in regulation.

Bandon Trails, Hole 2. Judge the wind for club selection on this 214-yard (196-metre) par 3, which has bunkers on the left side of the green.

Old Macdonald, Hole 15. 'Westward-Ho', a 535-yard (489-yard) par 5, sees you hitting to an elevated green with a bunker just short of it on the right side of the fairway.

Barnbougle Dunes /
Lost Farm

Tasmania, Australia

Barnbougle Dunes / Lost Farm

Location: 425 Waterhouse Rd, Bridport, Tasmania, 7262, Australia

Website: www.barnbougle.com.au

Phone number: 61 3 6356 0094

Sitting on the north-east coast of Tasmania near the quaint fishing village of Bridport, Barnbougle Dunes/Lost Farm has established itself as a golf destination of the highest calibre. Both golf courses make the most of the dune-land they are built on – in classic Scottish-links style, they use the natural features of the land. Both fairways and greens follow the undulations of the land. This means you'll often be playing approach shots either above or below your feet. It's also a true challenge to two-putt if you don't get your ball close on approach as the surface rises and falls. Cavernous bunkers protect greens or threaten tee shots along the fairways.

Between October and December, the trade winds known as the Roaring Forties power through Bass Strait, between Tasmania and mainland Australia. The courses are designed with these strong winds in mind, often playing into the prevailing north-westerly and sometimes playing downwind.

Barnbougle Dunes, which was designed by American Tom Doak and Australian Michael Clayton, offers narrower tee shots and smaller greens than Lost Farm, which generally has wider landing areas to aim at with your driver. The dunes are taller here, with the fairways often laid out like carpet at the base of these.

Interestingly, Lost Farm features 20 playable holes. Renowned US architects Bill Coore and Ben Crenshaw presented two holes to finish the regular 18 holes, but both were embraced and built. The course is a short drive to the east and is separated by the meandering Great Forester River.

The golf courses are situated in a spectacular location – with golden beaches on one side next to Bass Strait and gorgeous farmland on the other, giving a true sense of being in the dune-land ecosystem. Simply put, this is one of the most beautiful places in Australia. Wallabies and kangaroos roam around the farmland and a variety of shorebirds nest on the sand of the beach, such as the Hooded Plovers and Fairy Terns. The dunes are also home to tiger snakes, which is something to consider when searching for a lost ball. I almost stood on a frightened echidna (a spiky, egg-laying mammal) as I tried to take a photo of the beach setting.

The property was developed by Tasmanian farmer Richard Sattler, who grows potatoes and raises cattle on the 15,000-acre (6,070-hectare) property. Sattler runs both the golf courses and the farm with his family.

The vision he showed in building two of the finest golf courses in the world is

OPPOSITE: Barnbougle Dunes Course.

remarkable. The Bridport locals thought he was either crazy or having a mid-life crisis when he decided to go ahead with the investment.

'They don't quite say it as often now,' the stocky and affable farmer told me in the clubhouse after I finished my round. 'I'm having the last laugh.'

Sattler was convinced by American golf resort developer Mike Keiser, owner of Bandon Dunes, that the site was perfect for golf. And he knew the development was going to work out shortly before Barnbougle opened in December 2004. After inviting a local golfer to try the links out he got a glowing response following his round.

''That was better than sex' he said after dropping his bag down.'

Golf Digest ranked Barnbougle Dunes No. 33 in the world in 2016 and Lost

When to play: Year-round. Most challenging period is October to December, when the prevailing north-westerly wind is strongest.

Par: Barnbougle Dunes 71. Lost Farm 78

Yardage: Barnbougle Dunes 6,723 yards, 6,148 metres. Lost Farm 7,101 yards, 6,493 metres

Slope: Barnbougle Dunes 132. Lost Farm 132.

Rating: Barnbougle Dunes 72. Lost Farm 73.

Best hole: Barnbougle Hole 8 is a great example of how the course has embraced the natural contours of the land. At 448 yards (446 metres) off the back tee, it is also truly difficult par 4, with a giant grass-covered

mound splitting the fairway. The second shot is to an elevated green that is protected by a steep escarpment – it takes a solid drive and then a towering fairway wood to climb up to the level of the green. Lost Farm Hole 4 has a massive bunker, typical of the course, directly in front of the green, and another you can potentially hit in to on the left if you go into the first trap. The tee offers a beautiful view of the river and the beach.

The pro says: 'Absolutely stunning. I think that this is not only one of Australia's best, it is one of the best courses in the world, old or new.'
–Geoff Ogilvy on Barnbougle Dunes*

Farm at No. 40. Australian Golf Magazine has previously ranked them the No. 1 and No. 2 public access courses in Australia, respectively.

'You do your homework, you build it properly and you go for it,' Sattler says. 'You've got to have a backbone, not a wishbone.'

The challenges

Barnbougle Dunes and Lost Farm offer a true challenge for the amateur golfer when the wind is up; it can howl here. If you don't control your ball, it will sail away into the thick marram grass and be lost. The undulating greens are tricky to read, too. Most of them are elevated, making the challenge more difficult. Both fairways are a mix of fescue and bentgrass, and it is cut close so you'll need to have a top short game to chip or pitch with enough spin to hold the greens. It's advisable to play bump-and-run shots using a hybrid or seven-iron, or simply putt up onto the greens.

The resort experience

This is a more focused golf destination without all the side-line attractions of other resorts, and it's one of the best-value resorts you'll find. Barnbougle Dunes and Lost Farm are widely regarded as two of the best public access golf courses in Australia and their reputation is attracting keen golfers – individuals, couples and groups – from all over the world. And the golfers keep coming back, too, according to owner Richard Sattler, who says '80 per cent of our business is repeat'.

Dine and wine

Lost Farm Restaurant is the perfect place to relax and take in a stunning view of both the course and coastline from one of the highest points on the property. At sunset, this is one truly memorable place to enjoy a meal. The owners pride themselves on using fresh, locally-sourced vegetables, meat and seafood. I savored the entrée of slow-baked Tasmanian scallops, served in Mornay sauce and bread crumbs and Parmesan. The 'fries' on the side plate were more like whole potatoes. That was accompanied by a delicious local wine.

The accommodation

Barnbougle Dunes offers some 3.5-star cottages for those on a tighter budget as well as some upmarket villas, each featuring four executive bedrooms and full kitchen. The Lost Farm Lodge feels more like a stylish hotel, with either a double or single-queen suite. Enjoy the balcony view of the course and farmland all the way to the start of Tasmania's Sidling Range mountain range – it's the perfect way to relax into the evening.

OPPOSITE: Lost Farm course; *ABOVE:* Barnbougle Dunes Course

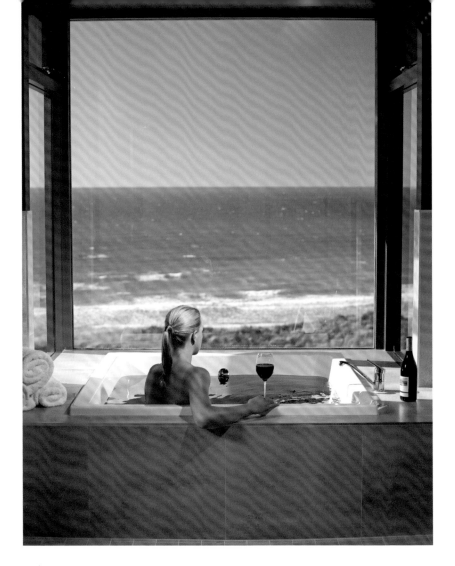

Other activities

The Barnbougle Spa offers a variety of packages to help you unwind and renew the body and the spirit, which may be needed if you've lost a lot of golf balls in the dunes. They include facials, massages and a vitality spa, where couples can soak together and sip on a local wine. You'll also find a naturopath and even childbirth education classes.

Barnbougle also hosts an annual polo event in January, in the lead up to which you can actually learn how to play. I also recommend dropping into one of the nearby vineyards for some wine tasting on your way up from Launceston airport.

*Source: barnbougle.com.au/play/the-dunes/about/

ABOVE: Lost Farm Lodge's Magnesium Pool; *BELOW:* Barnbougle Interiors.
OPPOSITE: Lost Farm view from the vitality spa.

The Bluffs Ho Tram, Hole No. 1.

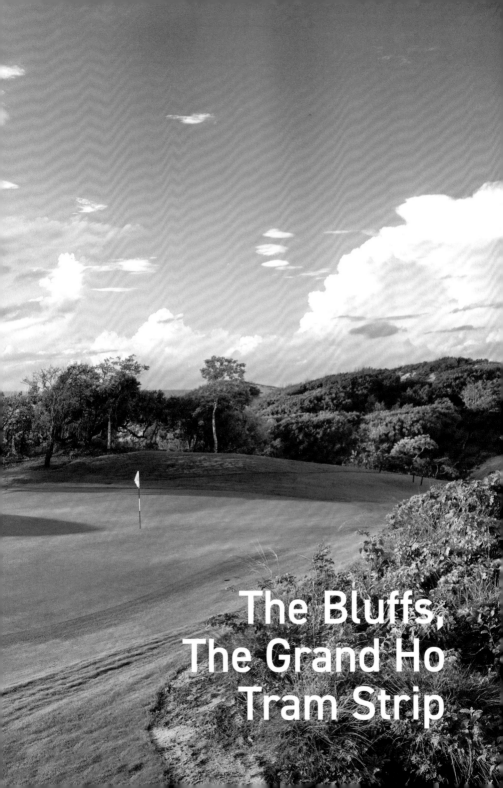

The Bluffs,
The Grand Ho
Tram Strip

The Bluffs, The Grand Ho Tram Strip

Location: Phuoc Thuan, Xuyen Moc, Ba Ria – Vung Tau, Vietnam
Website: thebluffshotram.com
Phone number: 84 64 378 8666

The Bluffs is a stunning links-style course on the south-eastern coast of Vietnam approximately two and a half hours' drive to the south-east of Ho Chi Minh City. It was designed by Australian golfing legend Greg Norman and opened in 2014 with a game between New Zealander Michael Campbell, Englishman Robert Rock, Vietnamese star Tang Thi Nhung and rising local amateur Ng Bao Nghi. Campbell was impressed with the layout.

'I've played a lot of courses around the world and this (one) is as good as it gets,' he said.*

The golf resort, which features the luxurious hotel The Grand, is emblematic of how golf is growing in stature in Vietnam. The course plays host to the Ho Tram Open – one of the country's richest sporting events – on the Asian Tour in March.

Adopting an approach of least disturbance to the sand dunes it is built on, Norman embraced the site's natural features – vegetation, rocks, streams and undulating topography – to create each hole.

'This is one of only two pieces of land of this quality and character I have ever been given to work with – the other being Doonbeg [in Ireland],' Norman said in a statement published by the course. 'I'm a firm believer in using what Mother Nature gives us on a particular site. This one has it all.'

The result is outstanding – The Bluffs was named 'World's Best New Golf Course' at the 2015 World Golf Awards in Portugal, *Golf Digest* ranked it No. 74 in its list of the *World's 100 Greatest Golf Courses 2016–17* and Japanese golf writer Masa Nishijima rates it as the second-best golf resort in Asia.

To give you an idea of the challenge, the 257-yard (235-metre), par-3 15th plays uphill to the highest part of the golf course, with sandy waste area all the way to the left side of the green. It's worth taking in the ocean views once you get there.

The Bluffs clubhouse is impressive, too – a 24,757-square-foot (2,300-square-metre) building that features the five-star Infinity restaurant, spacious lockers and a balcony that overlooks the back nine and the East Sea.

'This site is also more elevated (than most), which offers more dramatic views and also brings the wind into play more,' Norman said. 'Wind was definitely one of the most significant factors in designing the course, especially since the direction changes

OPPOSITE: The Bluffs course – Hole No. 5.

180 degrees for several months during the year. It affected nearly every decision, from the initial layout of the holes to fairway widths and irrigation coverage. Fortunately, we were able to create a good balance of holes for it.'

The challenges
Classic links-style shotmaking with natural undulations, blind shots around the large sand dunes and a mix of jungle vegetation and sandy wasteland if you miss the fairways.

The resort experience
After you wrap up your round, it's time to head back to The Grand – a 541-room five-star luxury hotel. The rooms are elegant, the buffet breakfast is included and the room service is 24 hours, but it's the activities that stand out here. This place looks like an absolute hoot to visit. It's perfectly positioned next to the sandy beach and has a bunch

Type of grasses: The greens are Tif-Eagle Bermuda, and the tees, fairways and rough are Bermuda 419.

When to play: The course is open year around but will play longer during the wet season (from April to September) as opposed to the dry season (October to March). The course is closed for maintenance on Tuesdays.

Par: 71

Yardage: 7,007 yards; 6,408 metres

Slope: 131

Rating: 74.4

Best hole: Hole 10 will test even long hitters with 651 yards (595 metres) to the green.

The par 5 plays downhill off the tee, before leveling out, and can then be attacked in several ways.

The designer says: 'Playing true links golf among the dunes of southern Vietnam and having dramatic ocean views throughout your round will make The Bluffs Ho Tram Strip one of the most unique golf experiences in the world.' – Greg Norman *

The pro says: 'It's a seaside course, naturally carved through sand dunes. The elevation changes provide for some extremely dramatic views. The course has two distinct wind directions, which can be very strong in the dry season.' – Patrick Kelly, Head Professional of features for kids (or the young at heart) such as the huge Dragon Slide that carries you into the pool (for kids 12 and up), putt-putt golf, an arcade-style game centre, and the Grand Cinema with movie screenings, all complimentary for guests. The Grand Central Park has football, basketball and a kids' playground, too. However, I may have to stay away from the Jukebox Karaoke, depending on how brave I feel – there are individual rooms for those inclined.

Dine and wine
You might have to walk the course after touring the eateries – every palate is catered for here with 11 restaurants and bars to choose from, including two gourmet facilities: Ju Bao Xuan, which serves up Cantonese cuisine, and The Grand Bistro, which offers French-crafted fare including steaks and fresh seafood. I'm going to try the fresh seafood at Ginger, which specializes in traditional Vietnamese dishes, and 8 Dragons, which has Chinese noodles and Korean fare. Afterwards, I might settle back with a whiskey in hand at Club 9, a nightclub with dancing into the early hours.

The accommodation
There are six different types of rooms to choose from, starting with the Grand Double (with two double beds) all the way through to the Premier Ocean View Suite, with two bathrooms, a fridge and microwave, lounge room and stunning outlook over Ho Tram Beach. Expect double marble vanities, tubs and showers in the bathrooms. Hopefully you'll enjoy the views over the dunes, the course and the East Sea on the balcony instead.

TOP: The Grand Hotel Pool.
OPPOSITE LEFT: The Grand Hotel and Beach, *OPPOSITE RIGHT:* The Grand Hotel

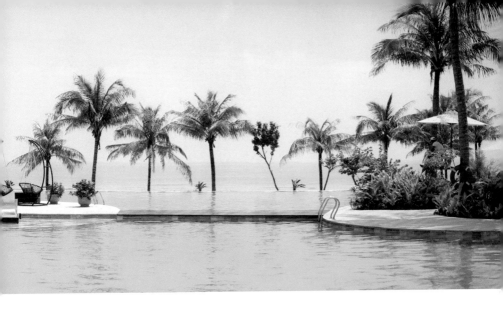

Other activities

As well as the previously mentioned kids' activities, it is hard to go past the fun on Ho Tram Beach. The beach services team can fix you up with a surfboard, body board, stand-up paddle board or kayak. There is beach-side yoga, too. Other facilities include a fitness centre, Kids' Corner (with daily activities such as crafts and tennis) and spa. More adventurous types can take the Minh Dam Tour, a half-day outing that takes in historic sites at Minh Dam Mountain.

*Source: thebluffshotram.com

Cabot Links

Nova Scotia, Canada

Cabot Links

Location: 15933 Central Avenue, Inverness, Novia Scotia, B0E 1N0, Canada
Website: cabotcapebreton.com
Phone number: 1 855 652 2268

Set along a golden beach on the windswept western coast of Novia Scotia, a stunning retreat for the serious golfer lies waiting. Cabot Links is focused on its courses – Cabot Links and Cabot Cliffs – which are set on dramatic coastal clifftops and alongside a two-mile-long beach in the remote village of Inverness, Cape Breton in far east Canada. It is the most talked about new golf resort in the world over the past five years, according to Canadian golf writer Dave Finn.

'When opened in 2012, Cabot Links was Canada's only authentic links course,' Finn said. 'Using the site of an old coal mine, architect Rod Whitman created a magnificent 18-hole, par-70 course. Six holes play directly along the coastline, and every other hole overlooks the Gulf of St Lawrence.

'Cabot Links is both stunning and challenging, with fescue galore. Rule No.1 – keep it on the fairway. Rule No. 2 – bring lots of balls. The greens, averaging over 45 yards (41 metres) deep, are so large that you are actually allowed to take pull carts on them.'

The goal for architects Whitman for Cabot Links and Bill Coore and Ben Crenshaw for Cabot Cliffs (which was completed in 2016), was to create true links courses as seamlessly as possible using the coastal environment. They embraced the natural contours of the sandy-soiled land to build undulating fairways and greens as well as spectacular elevated tees.

There's a variety of terrain at Cabot Cliffs as well as some severe elevation changes. You'll play past the beach, sand dunes, cliff tops, pine forest and meandering rivers. The beauty was overwhelming for *Golf Digest's* Ron Whitten who felt 'giddy' on the ninth.

'Midway through my maiden round at Cabot Cliffs . . . I'd already played through four landscapes, from highlands to river valley to sand dunes to pine trees and was now standing on the ninth tee, facing a short iron downhill to a cliff-edge green backdropped by the shimmering Gulf of St Lawrence.'

Cabot Cliffs and Cabot Links both made *Golf Digest's* list of the *Top 100 Golf Courses in the World 2016–17*, coming in at 19 and 93 respectively.

OPPOSITE: Cabot Cliffs Course.

The challenges

Embrace effective links-style play to keep the score down on both courses. The windy conditions mean you should keep the ball trajectory down, hit bump and runs and putt from off the green where necessary. Some of the greens are enormous here, so three putting is not always a bad result. Caddies are also available to help with local knowledge.

The resort experience

Golfers are in for a truly memorable couple of rounds at Cabot Links, but the resort is built to enhance the experience. There are beautiful views of the Gulf of

Type of grasses: Greens, fairways, tees and rough are all fescue grass of varying length.

When to play: Being in north-east Canada, the golf season runs from early May until late October between the chilly winter.

Par: Cabot Links: 70, Cabot Cliffs: 72

Yardage: Cabot Links: 6854 yards, 6267 metres Cabot Cliffs: 6764 yards, 6185 metres

Slope: Cabot Links: 132. Cabot Cliffs: 144

Rating: Cabot Links: 73.7. Cabot Cliffs: 74.3

Best hole: Cabot Cliffs' 16th hole (176 yards, 161 metres) is one of the most picturesque holes in Canada. It's an intimidating tee shot

to a green that has ocean cliff on all but the left side, and the flag position and wind will determine how you play it. For Cabot Links, the long 6th is another much-photographed hole, with views of the harbour on the left side of the dog-leg par 4 and behind the infinity green. Another postcard moment.

The general manager says: 'What really sets the courses apart is how the landscape lended itself so naturally to golf ... Another important aspect of both courses is their playability. The courses are playable for high handicappers but are also very challenging for competitive and professional golfers alike.'
– Andrew Alkenbrack

St Lawrence from both the main hotel rooms and the separate villas. Golfers will find three restaurants to choose from as well as a café in the town. The resort sits in the quiet town of Inverness, along the vaunted Cabot Trail, a spectacular 185-mile (298-kilometre) road-trip that loops through Cape Breton Highlands National Park.

Dine and wine

Expect fresh seafood at the restaurants here. Guests can often watch the lobster boats arrive back and then order something from the haul later. The Panorama Restaurant (upscale dining featuring ocean views) and Cabot Bar (casual fare, fine wines and whiskies) overlook Cabot Links' 18th green and have tremendous views of the entire course.

The accommodation

Designed by Nova Scotia architect Susan Fitzgerald and interior designer Alexandra Angle, the 72-room Cabot Links Lodge was constructed using local timber and cedar. The rooms offer floor-to-ceiling ocean views and all the modern creature comforts are included inside, such as Italian Terry robes, rainfall showers, Wi-Fi, 46in TVs and pillow-top beds. Rooms start at the Cabot Double, which has a sitting area with lounge chair, writing desk and credenza, through to the more luxurious Deluxe King Balcony with king bed and outdoor terrace.

Bigger groups may opt for the two-bedroom and four-bedroom Villas, which also

ABOVE: Cabot Links, OPPOSITE ABOVE: Cabbot trail horseback riding; OPPOSITE LEFT: Fly-fishing in the Margaree Valley; OPPOSITE RIGHT: Links Cabins.

offer majestic views of Cabot Links as well as the ocean. You'll get your own kitchen and private deck. Families can also rent four- and five-bedroom residences a short distance from the resort.

Other activities

This is a playground for outdoors types. Try horseback riding, fly fishing, whale watching, kayaking, deep-sea fishing or even learning a traditional Cape Breton square dance. I can see myself doing that after taking a nearby whisky distillery tour. For the more romantic, let the resort pack you a picnic basket lunch and spend some special time overlooking the ocean together.

The Carrick /
Cameron House

Loch Lomond, West Dunbartonshire, Scotland

The Carrick / Cameron House

Location: Loch Lomond, West Dunbartonshire, G83 8QZ, Scotland, United Kingdom
Website: cameronhouse.co.uk
Phone number: 44 1389 310 777

The Cameron Club's championship golf course, The Carrick, overlooks Loch Lomond in one of Scotland's most scenic regions, The Loch Lomond and Trossachs National Park in the central part of the country. The course opened in 2007. Canadian architect Douglas Carrick designed a layout that works its way through the lowlands in the front nine, with trees lining the fairway and some holes playing adjacent to the lake or streams. After the 437-yard/400-metre, par-4 9th, you can enjoy some food and drinks at the Highland Laddie, a halfway house that was once a London River Thames boat. You just need to order ahead.

Then you'll be heading up to the highlands on the back nine, which sits on a ridge that overlooks the 3,196-foot (974-metre) Ben Lomond. The last few holes return to the clubhouse next to marshland by the lake. The designer has given the parkland golf a traditional links feel with how the bunkering is set up. European golf writer Jo Maes sums up the challenge for golfers: 'It's a tough track with deep bunkers and sweeping fairways. Greens are undulated and one rule to follow is that 'everything falls towards the loch'.'

The par-3 14th is a memorable one for both its trickiness and beauty, Maes said. 'With the tee box high up, it's hard to judge distance and, with danger front and left, the obvious bailout is right of the green, which then leaves a tricky chip. A lovely hole with the vast expanse of Loch Lomond in the back drop.'

The Carrick has hosted the Ladies Scottish Open (2007 and 2008), the PGA Cup (2009) and Europro Tour in 2014, 2015 and 2016. The Claret Jug serves as the 19th hole, where you can have some food or a beer after the round. Cameron House also has a nine-hole course called the Wee Demon in the grounds of the resort, which also has some fine lake views.

The challenges

Loch Lomond is a beautiful water hazard you are encouraged to play around. The many small, deep bunkers around the undulating greens combined with solid distance off the back tees keep it challenging. Pro's tip: 'The key is to hit the fairways and keep out of the bunkers, it's that simple!'

OPPOSITE: Seaplane.

The resort experience

Cameron House, a grand 18th-century baronial mansion, takes in some of Scotland's most striking scenery overlooking Loch Lomond. Located on the south side of the national park, the five-star hotel is less than 30 minutes' drive to the northwest of Glasgow. The destination was named 'Scotland's Best Spa Resort 2016' at the Scottish Outdoor Leisure Awards and 'Best Luxury Resort Spa for Scotland 2016' at the World Luxury Spa Awards, so you can imagine the pampering you'll get at the spa will be worth the short concierge transfer from the resort's main building. The spa has 17 treatments rooms, a steam room, Rasul mud chamber with steam room and a Relaxation Suite. The concierge will also organize the transfer to The Carrick golf course.

Back at the resort, it is worth taking a dip in the rooftop infinity pool, which is designed to give you a special view of the lake. Writer Jo Maes painted an attractive image of the surroundings.

'Enjoy an evening stroll along the bonny banks of Loch Lomond with the sound of bagpipes echoing across the gentle ripples caused by the passing boats before you retire to the bar and sip on one of the highland single malts Scotland is famous for.'

Dine and wine

Cameron House features five dining options for guests. The top pick could be Michelin-Star restaurant Martin Wishart at Loch Lomond, which has a menu that changes with the produce each season delivers. Some of the regular seafood includes

Type of grasses: Greens are a blend of bentgrass and annual meadow, while the fairways are a mix of fescue and rye grasses.

When to play: Year-round.

Par: 71

Yardage: 7,082 yards, 6,476 metres.

Standard Scratch Score: 74

Best hole: The signature hole is the 175-yard (160-metre) 14th, a par 3 that provides a spectacular view of Loch Lomond and Ben Lomond from a tee that sits 100 feet (30 metres) up on the hillside.

Orkney scallops west-coast brown crab. Wishart has also been awarded four AA Rosettes for its fine cuisine. Elsewhere, the elegant Cameron Grill restaurant has a salmon bar with smoked fish caught in local lochs, The Boathouse features wood-fired pizza, the Claret Jug takes care of the 19th hole, or enjoy a whisky at The Great Scots Bar. Afternoon tea is also served with freshly-baked scones and pastries or a flute of Moët.

The accommodation
The rooms are set out like a Scottish residence with traditional furniture, tartan patterns and bathrooms that feature monsoon showers and bespoke toiletries.

ABOVE: 15th Hole at The Carrick.

A Classic Room also comes with a signature bathrobe. On the more luxurious side, a Whisky Suite has a living room, master bedroom and bathroom, and some of the best views of Loch Lomond.

Other activities
There are two ways to see Loch Lomond: you can take a boat cruise on the Celtic Warrior from the Cameron House marina or, even better, hop in the seaplane that parks out the front of the hotel and go for a scenic flight. The resort's Leisure Club features squash courts, two swimming pools, a steam room and jacuzzi, plus a gym with over 50 fitness classes a week.

Cape Kidnappers, Holes 14, 15 & 16.

Cape Kidnappers

Hawke's Bay, New Zealand

Cape Kidnappers

Location: 446 Clifton Road, Te Awanga, Hawke's Bay, 4180, New Zealand
Website: www.capekidnappers.com
Phone number: Lodge 64 6 875 1900 Pro Shop: 64 6 873 1018

New Zealand offers so many beautiful locations to visit and this, I can confidently say, is one of its jewels. Set on luxurious farmland overlooking Hawke's Bay on the North Island, Cape Kidnappers offers an unforgettable luxury golf experience, especially for couples.

Renowned American golf architect Tom Doak embraced the rugged coastal features to provide a true challenge for both the amateur and professional golfer. Immaculately groomed fairways lay between deep ravines and bluffs. From the air, the fairways look like long green fingers that extend right to the edge of 460-foot (140-metre) cliffs above the Pacific on the back nine.

There is a real sense of being far away in the countryside as you play. Sheep and cattle roam the paddocks surrounding the course. Gannets soar above the cliff tops and their nearby nesting area – Cape Kidnappers plays host to one of New Zealand's largest mainland colonies of the bird, which migrate for breeding between September and May.

Cape Kidnappers features 6,000 acres (2,428 hectares) of spectacular rolling hills, pasture, pine forest and coastline cliffs. I reached for my camera as many times as for my driver.

The course is regularly included in the world's top 100 courses by the golf press (*Golf Digest* ranked it 16 in 2016 and *Golf Magazine* ranked it No. 40 in 2015) and it is easy to see why. The links-style layout makes the most of the natural setting, with holes defended by elevation changes as well as well-placed bunkers. Tall fescue grasses flank the fairways or ravines that are well and truly out of bounds.

American billionaire Julian Robertson clearly fell in love with New Zealand before building three luxury lodges there – The Farm at Cape Kidnappers, Kauri Cliffs (see page 108) in Northland and Matakauri in Queenstown. And you don't have to love golf to be overwhelmed by the five-star experience at Cape Kidnappers – the food, service and accommodation are outstanding.

The challenges
Whilst the lush fairways seem wide open, you'll do well to avoid well-placed bunkers off the tee and approaching the greens, especially if the wind picks up. Tall fescue grasses will swallow balls.

OPPOSITE: Cape Kidnappers Course.

The resort experience

In peak season, some 50 staff members cater for up to 56 guests at The Farm, which gives you an idea of the care given. I remember the personal and warm reception by The Farm's manager. One of my favorite spots was the solar-heated pool and spa where you can enjoy a stunning view of Hawk's Bay as you bathe.

Dine and wine

Gentlemen require a jacket for dinner in the Lodge, but don't panic if you left yours at home – they'll lend you one that fits. This rates as one of the finest dining experiences of my life. The evening starts with pre-dinner drinks, served with hot and cold canapés, then each course is paired with a wine, many from the local

Type of grasses: Tees and fairways are a mixture of Colonial bentgrass and fescue. The greens are creeping bentgrass.

When to play: Year-round. Warmer months attract the most players between October to April plus a higher green fee and accommodation costs. I'd be tempted to rug up and take the challenge on between May and September. There are some calm, warm days to be had during this period as well, according to Jon McCord, Cape Kidnapper's Head Professional.

Par: 71

Yardage: 7,119 yards, 6,510 metres

Best hole: Adam Scott* is said to love the 'Pirates Plank', the 650-yard (594-metre), par-5 15th for its stunning beauty and tough lay up as the fairway to the green narrows. There is a 459-foot (140-metre) cliff on the left and a 66-foot (20-metre) drop on the right side of the fairway. Miss your approach left and it sails into the Pacific Ocean. My favorite hole is 'Widow's Walk', the par-5 16th hole, mainly because of the crow's nest-like tee box, which sits far up on the cliff top. Almost vertigo inducing, it's unlike anything I've experienced before in golf and has a truly breathtaking view of the cliffs and the Pacific, and the course itself on the other side.

Hawke's Bay vineyards. The menu changes daily but features New Zealand beef and lamb, local seafood and vegetables grown in The Farm's own garden.

The accommodation

The Farm's suites and cottages offer five-star luxury and all the creature comforts you could want. The Ridge Suite is one of the most smartly-designed apartments my wife and I have stayed in. For example, a plasma television is concealed behind a painting, like a safe. It's both cozy and spacious, and features a giant bathtub to soak in.

Other activities

Enjoy the great outdoors with some clay target shooting. An instructor will guide you through the technique of how to take aim and pick off the targets as they are launched out across the Pacific Ocean. There are plenty of walks to enjoy the picturesque scenery, including one to Kanuka Block, or take a mountain bike out to explore the trails across the 6,000-acre (2,428-hectare) property. Otherwise you can go on a guided horse ride or be taken on a Can-am all-terrain vehicle tour.

After that, unwind in the The Lodge's Spa, which features facials, massage, foot reflexology, pedicures, body wraps, hair care and manicures. Perfect.

*Source: www.capekidnappers.com/PicsHotel/CapeKidnappers/Brochure/2015/GAFeb15_024.pdf

ABOVE: Cape Kidnappers Course.

OPPOSITE TOP: On the green. MIDDLE: Pool and Cabana; BOTTOM: The Lodge.

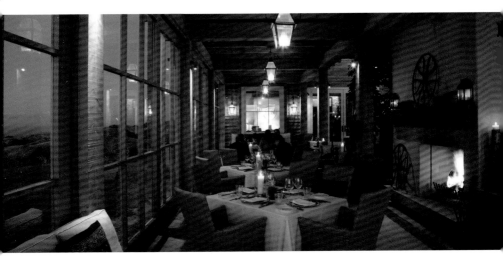

The designer says: 'The surface is firm and fast, the conditions can be windy, and the player who can control his trajectory will be master of the course. If you stray on your approaches, you'll actually hope to get caught up in bunkers hanging off the green's edge, some of them deeper than you've ever seen before. At the 6th and 15th holes, it's possible to pull your approach off the very end of the earth, though it will take nearly ten seconds of hang time for your ball to reach the ocean below.' – Tom Doak *

Cape Wickham, Hole No. 10.

Cape Wickham Links

Tasmania, Australia

Cape Wickham Links

Location: Cape Wickham, King Island, Tasmania, 7256, Australia
Website: capewickham.com.au
Phone number: 61 3 6463 1200

When it comes to finding the perfect spot to create a links course, you might have to go roam to unfrequented territory. That is just what Australian developer Duncan Andrews has done with Cape Wickham Links, which can be found on the north-west coast of King Island in Bass Strait. The remote patch of land sits between Victoria and Tasmania, exposed to the famous 'Roaring Forties' trade winds that blow hard from the west that sailing ships once harnessed. Australian golf writer Darius Oliver spotted the dramatic stretch of Australian coastline and immediately knew the potential of the site. He convinced Andrews to build a world-class course there. Andrews brought in American architect Mike DeVries, who, with Oliver, designed the course in 2015.

Oliver explained what he saw in the site this way: 'After seeing more than 1,500 golf courses worldwide, I stumbled upon Cape Wickham on King Island and instantly recognized it to be the most beautiful golf site anywhere on earth. The property is unique for a number of reasons: the rugged cliffs, the jagged, irregular coastline, the constant and uninterrupted Bass Strait views, the towering dunes, the beach and north-facing Victoria Cove and the 150-foot stone Cape Wickham lighthouse. Beyond those dramatic physical features, are a gloriously walkable routing and an unmistakable aura that you feel as you traverse the various sections of the course.'

With a population of approximately 1,600 residents, King Island is not a major hub and you'll be flying in on a regional airline or charter as there are no ferry services – my advice is, the larger the plane, the better. However, golfers are making the journey to Cape Wickham to enjoy a course that has captured the attention of the golfing world. After opening in 2016, *Golf Digest* immediately ranked the links No. 24 in its list of *World's 100 Greatest Courses – 2016–2017* and *Australian Golf Digest* ranked it No. 3 in the country.

The first five holes work across Cape Farewell headland (watch out for seals on the rocks near the hole 2 green), holes 6 to 13 incorporate the dune land to the south of the cape, and the final five holes head towards the Lighthouse and Victoria Cove.

With eight holes running next to the ocean, two greens and three tees by the shoreline and a dramatic 18th that bends around the beach at Victoria Cove that is in play, I can almost taste the salt from the sea spray.

OPPOSITE: Cape Wickham Hole No. 16.

Golf Digest's Ron Whitten described the breathtaking layout at Cape Wickham this way: 'Its routing is heart-pounding, starting along rocks and crashing surf, moving inland but not out of the wind, returning to ocean edge at the downhill 10th, pitch-shot 11th and drivable par-4 12th, then wandering into dunes before a crescendo closing hole curving along Victoria Cove Beach, which is in play at low tides.'

The challenges

Undulating fairways, wild-looking bunkers, forced carries over valleys and ridges as well as large greens make this a tough course. A howling wind from the south-west will make it truly challenging. A wind jacket is recommended.

The resort experience

Cape Wickham's golf course is the drawcard here with the resort itself being in its infancy. This destination is purely for golfing parties and individuals who want to play a unique and brilliant course. There are 16 rooms that take advantage of the

Type of grasses: Fescue on tees, fairways and greens.

When to play: The course is open all year, but it gets coldest between June and September and the Roaring Forties blow strongest between October and December if you are after a true golfing test.

Par: 72

Yardage: 6,725 yards, 6,149 metres

Best hole: The par-4 18th is a beauty. The fairway follows the curve of Victoria Cove Beach and players are invited to cut the dogleg from the tee with the beach being in bounds. It might be the world's longest bunker. It's then about landing the ball on a thin green.

location with balconies that overlook Cape Wickham Lighthouse, Victoria Cove Beach or the golf course. There are daily flights to King Island from Melbourne's airports as well as Launceston and Burnie in Tasmania. Once there, you can book a bus transfer or hire a car from the airport for the 30-minute drive to Cape Wickham.

Dine and wine

You can go to the Clubhouse restaurant for something hot. The lunch menu includes burgers, steak sandwiches, Aussie meat pies and crayfish risotto. I'll be choosing a King Island eye fillet or Atlantic salmon for dinner there. King Island boasts some highly sought-after produce – including lobster, cheeses, beef, oysters and vegetables – that all find their way onto restaurant menus.

The accommodation

The lodging is comfortable but modest. Each air-conditioned room (366 square feet, 34 square metres) features an en suite bathroom, two single beds, a fridge, TV and Wi-Fi. Ceiling-to-floor windows take advantage of some beautiful views.

Other activities

The trade winds can produce some good swells out of Bass Strait so it shouldn't come as a surprise that there are some great surf breaks on the quiet beaches, including Victoria Cove. The most famous surf spot here is Martha Livinia Beach, which is less than 30 minutes away. King Island also offers anglers some great fishing, either from the shore or on charter boats, where you can hook a snapper, barracoota, or salmon.

ABOVE: View from rooms.

OPPOSITE ABOVE: Hole 18 fairway; LEFT: Lodge room view; RIGHT: Lodge room.

Casa de Campo, Teeth of the Dog course.

Casa de Campo

La Romana, Dominican Republic

Casa de Campo

Location: Carretera La Romana – Higuey, La Romana 22000, Dominican Republic
Website: www.casadecampo.com.do
Phone number: 1 809 200 1304

A trip to Casa de Campo Resort & Villas on the Dominican Republic's southeast coast will reward you with the opportunity to play three championship courses designed by World Golf Hall of Fame member Pete Dye. The development sits on some 7,000 acres (2,833 hectares) of pristine coastal land, with numerous holes sitting next to the azure waters of the Caribbean Sea.

The signature course is Teeth of the Dog, a 7,471-yard (6,831-metre) challenge that has been ranked the No. 1 golf course in Latin America and No. 39 in the world by *Golf Magazine* in 2015. It has also taken the title of the Caribbean's Best Golf Course 2014 at the World Golf Awards. When Dye spotted the beautiful and rugged piece of coastal land, he thought it was the perfect place for a golf course. However, it wouldn't have been much fun to carve out the rocks and coral by hand to make way for tees, fairways and greens before it opened in 1971. A Dominican crew of 300 used chisels, sledgehammers and pickaxes to do the work. They referred to the area as 'Dientes del Perro', or 'Teeth of the Dog' – and the name stuck. The course features seven Caribbean-edged holes and two extremely difficult par 3s (Holes 7 and 16).

Golfers must also play Dye Fore, a 27-hole course that has seven cliff-side holes that drop some 300-feet (91 metres) to the Chavón River below on one side. It boasts two of the best par 3 holes you will play – holes 12 and 15 – as well as 360-degree views that take in the Dominican Mountains, the Caribbean Sea, the river and Casa de Campo Marina and Altos de Chavón artists' village. The course was renovated in August 2014 with Paspalum greens. In September 2011, the resort opened Dye Fore Lagos, an additional nine holes on the northeast side of the property. Five holes work around three large lakes including two par 3s with small greens.

Finally, The Links course provides classic links-style play reminiscent of Scotland. The course was built in 1976 but has since been renovated with Paspalum greens. The 6,900-yard (6310-metre) design is situated inland and features water hazards on five holes as well as multiple bunkers.

The challenges

Teeth of the Dog features seven Caribbean-edged holes, devilish doglegs, long fairway bunkers, small targets for greens as well as water hazards (lakes and ocean).

OPPOSITE: Casa De Campo.

Type of grasses: Teeth of the Dog and The Links: Bermuda fairways, and Paspalum greens and tees. Dye Fore: all Paspalum.

When to play: Year-round, although the rainy season stretches from late April until October.

Par: Teeth of the Dog – par 72; The Links – par 71; Dye Four – par 72.

Yardage: Teeth of the Dog: 7,471 yards, 6,831 metres. Dye Fore: 7,740 yards 7,077 metres. The Links: 6,900 yards, 6,309 metres.

Slope: Teeth of the Dog 145, Dye Four 134, The Links 126

Rating: Teeth of the Dog 75.9, Dye Four 77.0, The Links 72.6

Best hole: So many great ones to choose from, but Hole 8 on Teeth has arguably the trickiest green, while the green on Hole 5 is almost entirely surrounded by the Caribbean. Also recommended are Hole 11 on The Links and Hole 4 on Dye Fore, Marina side.

The designer says: 'Almost by accident, I saw before me the most beautiful seaside location for a golf course. Little did I realize that my wonderful discovery would be the start of a lifelong devotion to this Caribbean country and its warm, gracious people.' – Peter Dye*

The prevailing north-easterly trade winds can make it even more of a challenge. Teeth has two of the toughest par 3s in golf. Dye Fore has five holes with lakes in play and, being elevated, experiences winds gusting up to 40 miles (64 kilometres) per hour. The Links Course is situated inland and water comes into play on five holes, while grass roughs and multiple sand traps will provide ample challenge.

The resort experience

Casa de Campo Resort & Villas has been a favored tropical escape for the world's politicians, financial moguls and Hollywood stars. They might have been attracted by the spacious suites, hotel rooms or luxury villas, the huge choice of gourmet dining with seven restaurants and bars, or the diverse range of outdoor activities between daiquiris. Or it might just be about being surrounded by the warm service of the Dominicans. Being able to park their yacht in the 370-slip Marina & Yacht Club would be an added drawcard.

It's an idyllic setting, too, with the Chavón River winding its way to the Caribbean Sea. Come at the right time and you'll see Flamboyan trees blooming with fiery-colored flowers sitting next to lush bougainvillea.

Guests receive a four-passenger golf cart for their personal use to explore the property – which makes it easier to race between the many attractions such as Altos de Chavón, the replica Mediterranean village. Some great facilities can be found on the lush tropical grounds, including a 245-acre (99 hectare) Shooting Centre, Polo and Equestrian Centre, La Terraza Tennis Centre.

Casa de Campo has received more awards than can be mentioned here, but they are currently shining the trophy for the World's Leading Luxury Sports and Villa Resort 2016 from the World Travel Awards and the Caribbean's Best Golf Hotel 2016 gong they won at the World Golf Awards.

Dine and wine

I get excited about food so I might just put on weight at Casa de Campo. There are seven resort restaurants boasting a wide range of gourmet cuisine and fine wines and spirits. The idea of digging into fresh seafood at The Beach Club (run by The Maccioni Family of the renowned Le Cirque Restaurant in New York) as I enjoy the cool see breeze on Minitas Beach is particularly appealing. Other options include La Cana by II Circo (Mediterranean cuisine), Pubbelly Sushi (Japanese-inspired fare), Sophia's Bar & Grill (expect DJ and band), La Casita (Spanish cuisine, tapas), The 19th Hole (lunch overlooking Teeth of the Dog), the Lago Grill (Dominican cuisine) and La Piazzetta (Italian recipes).

The accommodation

The hotel rooms are comfortable and offer easy access to the main and lobby pools. The Classic, Garden, Oceanfront and Exclusive Villas offer another level of privacy and luxury with your own pool, and staff ready to serve breakfast.

Other activities

The water sports look particularly fun here. Try snorkeling next to Catalina Island, kayaking on the Chavón River, sailing a catamaran on the Caribbean, paddle surfing, or a half-day of trophy fishing out to sea. On land, after a spot of tennis, target shooting or polo, you'll want to explore Altos de Chavón – an artisan's village modeled after a 16th-century Mediterranean city with museums, boutique shops and a 5,000-seat Grecian-style amphitheatre, opened with the help of one Frank Sinatra in 1982.

*Source: planetgolf.com.au

OPPOSITE ABOVE: Coast holes; ABOVE: Altos De Chavon.

The Vintage Course, Hole 13.

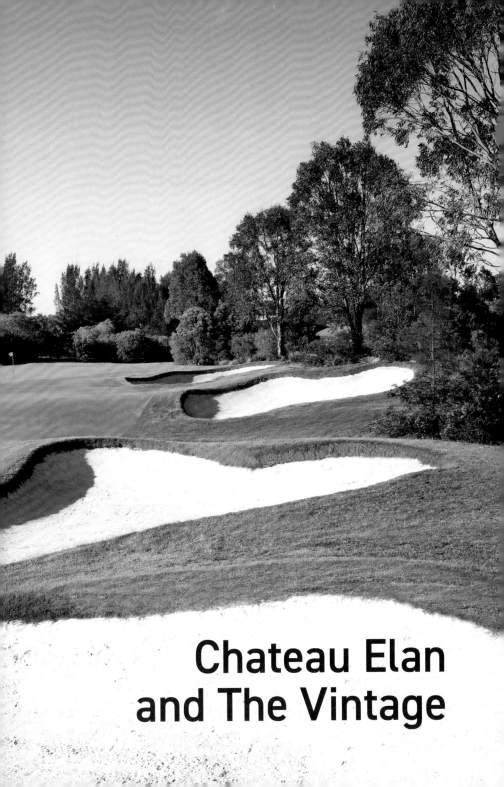

Chateau Elan
and The Vintage

New South Wales, Australia

Chateau Elan and The Vintage

Location: Vintage Drive, Pokolbin, NSW 2320 Australia
Website: chateauelan.com.au
Phone number: 61 2 4998 2500

The Vintage golf course and Chateau Elan are located near the small town of Pokolbin in the Hunter Valley, one of Australia's most famous wine regions. Approximately two and a quarter hours' drive north from the city of Sydney will see you amongst beautiful vineyards surrounded by the mountains of the Great Dividing Range. This is the setting of The Vintage, a course designed by Greg Norman and Bob Harrison in 2003.

The layout features undulating fairways, world-class bunkering, strategic par 4s, and slick bentgrass greens. It is a tale of two nines, according to Matt Farley, Director of Golf. 'The front nine being a challenging selection of par 4s and the back nine providing an interesting 'risk and reward' style of golf.'

There are a healthy variety of holes in play. The 389-yard (356-metre) hole 2 is a dogleg to the left that can be played using two irons. Thick woods surround the green. At 212 yards (194 metres), the par 3 8th will test you for distance and accuracy. There is water on the right and bunkers on the left of the green so you can easily be punished here. On the par-5 7th, you'll be playing through the vineyards as you climb a steep hill before hitting down to a fast green. If you miss left, your ball may end up in the neighboring winery. It's a beautiful hole, Farley said.

'The 7th hole is the most picturesque, as it runs amongst a vineyard, and the 9th boasts the Norman signature of having the native Australian gum trees to welcome you as you approach the tee.'

On the back nine, long hitters will be tempted to go for the green off the tee on some of the shorter par 4s, such as holes 13 and 16, but may want to think twice about taking on the par 5s – holes 10 and 14. You'll be hitting over water on the 187-yard (171-metre) par 3 12th, too.

It's cheaper to play The Vintage mid-week. I had a lovely round of golf here, perhaps thinking about the wine and cheese I was about to consume.

The challenges

Avoid the deep bunkers surrounding the greens as well as the gum trees. You'll have to navigate around or over lakes on holes 3, 8, 12, 15, 16 and 17. Pro's tip: 'Play consistent in the first six holes and then just enjoy the risk factor!'

OPPOSITE: Vintage Golf Course.

The resort experience

Chateau Elan is a luxury getaway that features villas spread out along the fairway of The Vintage golf course's 10th hole. Set on 100 acres (40 hectares) and surrounded by wineries, it is the perfect escape for golfers and wine lovers. And being just over two hours' drive from Sydney, it is not too hard to get to either. The creamy main building may not look like an ancient French chateau but it has chic interiors and, as well as featuring the lobby, houses a spa and salon with 17 treatment rooms plus spa suites for those who want to stay as close to the relaxing therapy as possible. The smartly dressed staff have been well recognized for their five-star service. The resort was Tripadvisor's Excellence Winner in 2015 as well as taking the NSW Tourism Awards of NSW Housekeeper of the Year 2016, Gold; Hall of Fame Luxury Accommodation in 2015; and Gold – Best Luxury Accommodation in 2013.

Dine and wine

The Hunter Valley is one of Australia's most famous wine regions. The cheese is grand as well. You must take a wine tour and sample drops from such famous brands as Brokenwood, Tempus Two, Tyrrell's and McGuigan Brothers at cellar door tastings. But you can also expect to enjoy great wines at the resort. Chateau Elan has four

Type of grasses: The fairways and greens are Santa Ana Couch turf and the rough is bentgrass.

When to play: Year-round.

Par: 71

Yardage: 6,826 yards, 6,242 metres

Slope: 147

Rating: 73

Best hole: A toss-up between the long par-3 8th (212 yards, 194 metres), which has water on the right and two bunkers on the left of the green, and the par-5 7th, which sees you hitting next to a vineyard.

The pro says: 'Each hole design is stamped with the classic Greg Norman signature of commence with a challenging tee, and the vital positioning and design of bunkers to ensure the golfer is thinking from the word go.' – Matt Farley, Director of Golf restaurants and two bars for visitors to choose from. The Legends Grill has select cuts from pasture- and grain-fed cattle. It also received the NSW Wine List's Restaurant & Catering Award for Best Wine List 2016. The next time I visit, I'll be starting with some Nelson Bay Rock Oysters, then moving to a Riverine Angus T-bone from the grill and finishing with white chocolate and raspberry rippled cheesecake.

You can also head to Café at Legends for light lunch overlooking the 18th green, The Vintage Yum Cha for some dim sims, Spike Bar & Café for a beer on tap, or Bar 1820 in the lobby of the Chateau Elan, which boasts a huge collection of Johnnie Walker Scotch Whiskies.

ABOVE: The 7th hole at the Vintage Golf Course; *BELOW:* Chateau Elan.

The accommodation

There are four luxury lodging options to choose from. The Spa Suite gives guests easy access to the spa and salon in the main building. The 646-square-foot (60-square-metre) lodgings feature a plinth-mounted spa bath, HDTV, Wi-Fi, and an Ergomotion king-size bed with in-built massage. I'm intrigued by what the 'zero-gravity' function on this bed does. You'll also get a balcony overlooking the course or a courtyard.

A one-bedroom villa (1033 square feet, 96 square metres) looks out on the 10th hole's fairway. It features a kitchen, dining area, lounge room, gas fireplace and balcony or terrace. The bathroom has a spa bath and separate shower. You can get a king-size bed or two king-size singles.

Other activities

As well as enjoying a massage in the spa there are some great activities to do in the Hunter. Take a bus tour to the boutique wineries or cheese makers; ride through the Molly Morgan Range on horseback on a guided trail ride with Hunter Valley Horse Riding; or take a horse-drawn carriage tour around the vineyards. I'll be going ballooning – you can watch sunrise high up over the Hunter and enjoy a buffet or champagne breakfast, too. Balloon Aloft and Beyond Ballooning offer these services. The Vintage has its own helicopter if you want to take a scenic flight or get transferred from Sydney's Mascot Airport, too. My experience of flying from Sydney – a route that takes you above the Harbour Bridge and the famous Opera House – to the Hunter was unforgettable.

The Datai
Langkawi

The Datai Langkawi

Location: Jalan Teluk Datai, 07000 Langkawi, Kedah, Malaysia
Website: thedatai.com/experiences/golf/
Phone number: 60 4 9500 500

The Els Club Teluk Datai is a majestic course set in a rainforest on the tropical island of Langkawi, which sits off the north-west coast of Peninsular Malaysia. The course was redesigned and relaunched by four-time major champion Ernie Els in 2014 and has already been named 'World's Best New Course' at the inaugural World Golf Awards.

Teluk Datai offers an exotic golf experience. The environment is simply stunning, with some holes playing towards the ancient rock of Mount Mat Chincang, which towers over the course. Other holes play towards the emerald waters of the Adaman Sea and next to gorgeous beaches with Thailand in the distance.

The fairways are like fine green carpets, laid out between dense rainforest – it's lush. The 18-hole, par-72 course plays 6,750 yards (6,172 metres). Most tees offer a reasonably wide landing zone for your driver. However, you are punished for poor ball control. There is no point searching for it in the second cut. As your caddie will tell you, 'It's a jungle ball' and you'll have to tee off again.

Ernie Els explained to me what he was aiming for when he redesigned the layout. 'We have some beautiful scenery there, on the banks of the Andaman Sea and adjacent to a tropical rainforest, so we wanted to configure the hole-routings to make the most of that,' he said. 'We also had the coastal road re-routed, which enabled us to have four holes that play right alongside the water, two on each nine. That's a wonderful little stretch of holes.

'Maybe the most distinctive design feature is the absence of bunkers, which is obviously pretty unusual for any golf course. It makes sense on a number of levels, though.

'As I said, the course is located in the middle of a rainforest so there is plenty of rainfall and that's probably the number one enemy in terms of bunker maintenance. So it has genuine practical benefits, but it also gave us some opportunities to be creative in other areas of the design; the use of trees in strategic areas, plus there's a stream that runs across the course and comes into play on several holes. So you don't miss the bunkers.'

I played the course in October – the end of the rainy season, which begins in March. It rains consistently during this period so you must watch for your windows for playing.

OPPOSITE: The Dining Room.

Many of the greens are elevated, keeping them dry, and the drainage on the fairways is remarkable. After belting rain, my shoes somehow stayed dry.

The putting surface changes speed depending on whether it is the rainy or dry season.

It gets hot out there in the jungle – a humid 84° Fahrenheit (29° Celsius) is typical in February. Sit out the front of the open-planned club house after your round and enjoy a cool drink and the great view of the course.

The challenges

Els removed the bunkers and brought in jungle hazards, trees and a fast-moving stream. There is a GPS course guide in the golf cart to give you a flyover of the hole, and distances to hazards and to the green. You must manage your game well to ensure you don't have a blowout hole.

And watch out for the cheeky and sometimes aggressive macaque monkeys, which have been known to pick up golf balls. Seriously, I had to chase a group of ten of them away with putter in hand next to the green on the 2nd hole.

Type of grasses: Zoysia matrella (known as Manila grass) on the tees and fairways, and TifEagle Bermudagrass on the greens.

When to play: The consistent rain during the wet season – between March and October – can make it harder to get on the course, but it is also cooler and less crowded.

Par: 72

Yardage: 6,760 yards, 6,181 metres

Slope: 120

Best hole: Dubbed 'Tranquility', Hole No. 6

offers a relatively narrow tee shot between trees that must be hit solidly. The approach shot to this 432-yard (395-metre) par 4 must carry a fast-moving stream that sits in front of a relatively small green after the fairway turns left.

The designer says: 'The holes that play alongside the water are very special, very memorable. Golfers are going to take a lot of photos there I think! I also like holes No.5 and No.17, which play to a double green; that's a really nice feature.' – Ernie Els

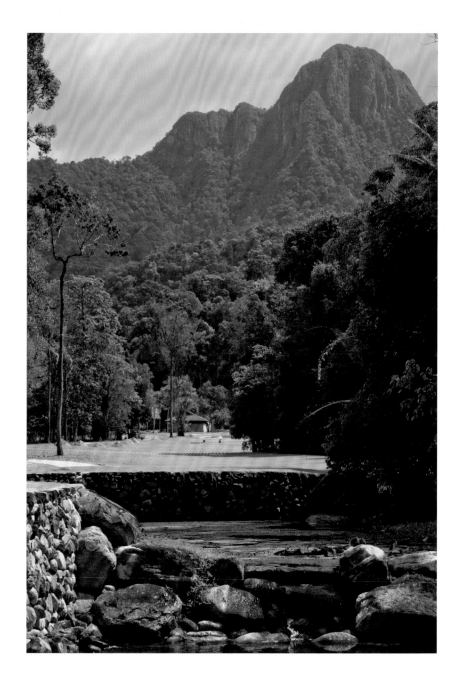

ABOVE: The Els Club Teluk Datai.
OPPOSITE LEFT: The Els Club; RIGHT: Superior villa bathroom.

The resort experience

The luxurious Datai Langkawi resort is a romantic and eco-friendly destination, which features four world-class restaurants and a superb Malaysian spa experience to help you unwind. The resort is built into a jungle with luxury bungalows spread out on the property so you have privacy. I was amazed at how many animals I saw at the resort – monkeys, boars, colugos, sea eagles, pied hornbills and many more. A clear stream winds its way through the resort, adding the tranquil sounds of running water to the soundtrack of the rainforest. The beach-side pool and bar is the perfect place to relax after a round of golf. The friendly staff will take care of your golf clubs as well as transfers to the course and airport, too.

Dine and wine

Datai Langkawi offers truly memorable culinary experiences. The Gulai House offers authentic Malay with Indian flavors for a romantic night in the rainforest. The Beach Club can take care of lunch with a wood-fired pizza or pool-side daiquiri. The Pavilion will make your eyes water with spicy and superb Thai, while the Dining Room has fresh fruits and omelets for breakfast, or Asian cuisine for dinner. Best to bring an appetite.

The accommodation

The Datai has 122 luxurious villas, suites and rooms spread out in the rainforest. One can stay near the canopy in the main building, tucked away deep in the jungle itself, or closer to a private beach. You'll enjoy a large air-conditioned room, a bathroom with double vanity and a giant tub. Sit back on the veranda and meditate to the sounds of the rainforest. A blissful and romantic retreat.

Other activities

Enjoy a soothing massage in the Datai Spa, which is set next to a bubbling brook and draws on the Malay concept of ramuan – gathering and mixing medicinal plants. Treatments go from 150 minutes through to 210 minutes and can feature aromatherapy foot polishes, a Dosha tea ceremony, deep-tissue massage or a 'love bath' with champagne for two.

One of my favorite experiences was taking the morning and evening nature walks with resident naturalist Irshad Mobarak. He explains about an amazing variety of plants and animal species in the rainforest, including frogs, dusky leaf monkeys, great hornbills, colugos (flying lemur), an acid-filled rengas plant and tongkat ali, whose boiled root is used as an aphrodisiac. This resort is teeming with life.

Stanley Thompson Course, Hole No. 4.

Fairmont
Banff Springs

Alberta, Canada

Fairmont Banff Springs

Location: 405 Spray Avenue, Banff, Alberta, Canada, T1L1J4
Website: www.fairmont.com/banff-springs/golf/
Phone number: 1 506 863 6310 / 1 800 720 825

Fairmont Banff Springs has two courses – the 18-hole Stanley Thompson and 9-hole Tunnel Mountain – laid out between huge mountains in the Banff National Park, a UNESCO World Heritage Site. The championship course was designed by Canadian Stanley Thompson in 1928 and it plays away from the famous Fairmont Banff Springs hotel, a grand building known as 'Canada's castle in the Rockies' that has been accommodating guests since June 1888. When Thompson was approached to build the course he said he had been asked to build the last word in golf, according to Steve Young, Director of Golf.

'The course was the first in the world to cost more than $US1 million to build,' Young said. 'When the first unofficial ranking of world golf courses came out, Banff was ranked No. 8 ahead of many prominent courses, including Winged foot, Pinehurst and Augusta National.'

The layout winds its way through a valley, and the fairways are relatively flat. The inward holes are laid out along the pristine Bow River. The bunkering is an outstanding feature of the design, being both strategic and aesthetically pleasing. The mountain scenery is the other stunning feature and Thompson made sure each hole made full use of the setting.

'He backdropped every hole with a scenic and grandiose background,' Young said. 'From 150 yards (137 metres), when you look at a golf green site you are inevitably looking up at a distant peak of a mountain.'

Perhaps the most unusual factor is that the Fairmont Banff Springs courses are built in a designated wildlife corridor. And there is plenty of wildlife nearby when you play, according to Young. 'If you stop and just listen you hear birds, running water and moving trees. If you are lucky you hear footfalls of animals, a warning or mating call, and even a chase scene.'

The course is closed between November 1 and April 30 when the wildlife has right of way. 'We get wolves, coyotes, elk and cougar travelling through the valley dominated by the golf course (bears are asleep).'

The Stanley Thompson Course ranked No. 4 in *ScoreGolf*'s list of *Canada's Best Public Golf Courses in 2015.*

OPPOSITE: Stanley Thompson Course, Hole No. 4, the 'Devil's Cauldron'.

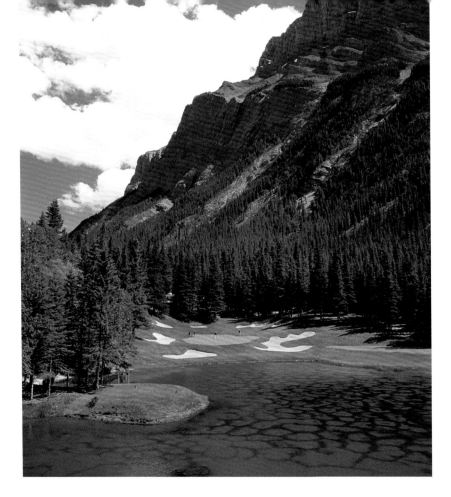

Type of grasses: Both courses use bentgrass on the greens, Kentucky bluegrass for the fairways and rough, with native fescue used as a framing grass.

When to play: As well as being a designated wildlife corridor in the colder months, the region sees a lot of snow in winter. The Stanley Thompson course is open on the second Friday in May through to the last weekend in September, depending on weather.

Par: Stanley Thompson Course 71 Tunnel Mountain Course 36

Yardage: Stanley Thompson Course 6,938 yards, 6,344 metres Tunnel Mountain Course 3,287 yards, 3,006 metres

Slope: Stanley Thompson Course 135 Tunnel Mountain Course 129

Rating: Stanley Thompson Course 72.9 Tunnel Mountain Course 70.4

The pro says: 'No housing, no highways, no airports, no unnecessary movement occurs while you play. It is therapeutic, rewarding, challenging and energising all at the same time. 18 unique holes that leave you wanting to return. 'My greatest piece of advice is that if you are not playing particularly well or mis-hit a shot, simply look up. The majestic beauty of the place and surroundings you are being afforded to play in should cure any ill feelings.' – Steve Young, Director of Golf

The challenges

Thompson built in risk-reward into many of the holes. The more direct approach will require flighting the ball over obstacles, mostly bunkers. The pro's tips: 'Adjust for elevation where it is present (holes 2, 4, 6 and 15) and remember you are playing a mile above sea level so your ball will fly farther in the lighter air.'

The greens are generous in landing area but fast. You'll have to putt well to score here. 'Know that greens break towards the river and that the grain of the greens runs away from the hotel.'

The resort experience

American golf writer Bob Fagan rates Fairmont Banff Springs as one of his top 10 golf resorts in the world and with good reason. 'Canada's castle in the Rockies' looks out on the majestic mountains next to the Alpine town of Banff, Alberta, which has plenty of restaurants and other attractions such as museums and galleries. There is an elegant look to the interiors that suits the classic architecture of the castle-like structure.

The luxury resort becomes a destination for skiers, snowboarders, dog sledders, snowshoers and ice skaters in winter but you can enjoy the European-style Willow Stream Spa all year. Here you can let your muscles relax as waterfalls wash over you and you bathe in a mineral pool. It was named Canada's No.1 Top Hotel Spa in *Travel+Leisure*'s World's Best Awards 2015. You might need it after enjoying a spot of tennis, some laps in the pool or horse riding. Everything from babysitting to bike storage is available at this five-star hotel.

Dine and wine

The Fairmont Banff Springs features an impressive 11 restaurants and bars to choose from. However, Stanley's Smokehouse comes highly recommended. The restaurant can be found at the championship golf course and has panoramic views of the fairways, Bow River and Canadian Rocky Mountains. The locals tell me the beef brisket, slow cooked over cherry wood for 18 hours, is a fine way to cap off a day of golf.

The accommodation

There are 764 guest rooms and suites on offer here. They range from a cozy Fairmont Room (150 square feet / 14 square metres) with a king-size bed and limited views through to the Royal Suite (1,500 square feet / 139 square metres) also with a king-size bed, but boasting 360 degree views of the Bow Valley and Canadian Rockies. The suite, which is located in the pinnacle of a castle peak, also comes with a grand piano (seriously), reception foyer, powder room, upstairs library and living room. It is fit for a king or queen no doubt.

Other activities

Banff is an outdoor wonderland, summer or winter. In the warmer months, besides the tennis and lap pool at the resort, you can sign up for river rafting, horseback riding, hiking or mountain biking. There's also the 'Kids' @ the Castle' club with activities such as arts and crafts plus a bowling and entertainment centre (including pool and table tennis) to enjoy at night.

ABOVE LEFT: indoor pool; *RIGHT:* lounging area.
OPPOSITE: view of the Fairmont from the fairway.

Best hole: There are many picturesque holes on the Stanley Thompson Course but No. 4 is the signature hole. Called 'Devil's Cauldron', it is one of Canada's most heralded par 3s and has recorded the most hole-in-ones at Banff Springs. Playing 192 yards (176 metres) from the back tee, you'll be hitting over a pond that is filled with water flowing from the mountains. If you miss the bunkers that surround the green, sloping banks will feed the ball onto the putting surface. Hole 5 is a thriller, too. The green is framed by Cascade Mountain behind it, while looking back at the tee you'll see a rock wall building up to the snowy Rundle Peak in the backdrop. It takes four solid shots to make par.

Montagu Course ~ Hole No. 10.

Fancourt

Fancourt

Location: Montagu Street, Blanco George, 6530, South Africa
Website: www.fancourt.co.za/en/home/
Phone number: 27 044 804 0000

Fancourt is set in the Western Cape's scenic Garden Route region – think stunning mountain ranges, forests, and beaches along the Indian Ocean – near the South African city of George. It is a golf resort with a historic heritage. The estate goes back to the construction of Manor House by Henry Fancourt White, a surveyor who helped build the Montagu Pass over the nearby Outeniqua Mountains, in the late 1880s. It wasn't until 1989 that Manor House was turned into a hotel and Fancourt a golf club by Helene and Andrea Pieterse.

Following that, German entrepreneur and keen golfer Dr Hasso Plattner and his wife Sabine bought and transformed the facilities in 1994, investing millions of rand to turn the estate into the premiere golfing destination it is today. *Golf Digest SA* editor Stuart McClean had no hesitation putting Fancourt at the top of his list of world's top golf resorts. Golfers can choose from three championship courses here: The Links, Montagu and Outeniqua.

The Links is the signature course and has been ranked No. 43 in the world by US edition of *Golf Digest*. South African golfing great Gary Player and Phil Jacobs designed the layout and converted an airfield into a links-style challenge with undulating fairways and narrow greens. It tries to echo the challenges of great links courses of the United Kingdom, including revetted pot bunkers to protect greens. The Links has hosted the 2005 South African Open, the 2003 Presidents Cup as well as the 2012 Volvo Golf Champions on the European Tour.

Montagu, the original course that Gary Player also designed, is another brilliant challenge for guests staying at Fancourt Hotel or Manor House. *Golf Digest SA* has ranked it the sixth best course in the country in 2016. Here you'll find a tree-lined layout with water hazards and its own undulating landscape to deal with.

You'll find the views of the Outeniqua Mountains impressive as you tee off on the aptly named third course – Outeniqua, which although similar to Montagu with plenty of water hazards, is an easier assignment for golfers. A 'stroke saver' provides distances to hazards and greens on all three courses.

The challenges
Players on The Links – the top course here – should watch out for the lakes and wetland as well as strategically-placed pot bunkers that guard narrow, slick greens. Montagu and Outeniqua both challenge golfers with water hazards and trees to avoid, but the former is by far the hardest challenge.

ABOVE: The Links – Hole No. 10.

The resort experience

Just a short drive from George Airport and you are in gorgeous countryside with the impressive Outeniqua Mountains in the background. The Fancourt resort sits on 1,515 acres (613 hectares) and aims to treat guests to a luxurious retreat in one of two hotel lodgings – the Fancourt Hotel or the historic Manor House.

Fancourt Hotel and Manor House both offer five-star services, with the latter providing butler-style attention for guests staying in its suites. But instead of being pampered all day, I'd be experiencing the many activities here. There's the indoor heated Roman Bath to talk politics in, indoor and outdoor pools, tennis courts, the golf academy, walking and cycling trails as well as birdwatching and fishing on the estate. After all that, you'd better get to the spa for a treatment such as the Roma Stone Placement Massage (a specialty using basalt rock).

Type of grasses: The Links' tees and fairways are a mixture of rye, fescue and bentgrass, with the greens being A4 bentgrass. Montagu/Outeniqua have Kikuyu tees and fairways as well as A1-A4 bentgrass greens.

When to play: Year-round, however, each of the three courses is closed for maintenance during the year for weeks at a time, so check the schedule before booking your trip.

Par: The Links 73, Montagu 72 and Outeniqua 72

Yardage: The Links 6,930 yards, 6,337 metres Montagu 6,714 yards, 6,140 metres Outeniqua 6,312 yards, 5,771 metres

Rating: The Links 74, Montagu 73 and Outeniqua 72

Best hole: The Links hardest hole is 'Sheer Murrrder', a 440-yard (402-metre) challenge that sees you hitting into the prevailing wind, trying to avoid a nasty bunker in the middle of the undulating fairway and staying away from the wetland on the left side. The green is flanked by two long bunkers. Montagu's par-5 18th is a fine challenge – big hitters might carry the three bunkers on the left side of the fairway. That will give them a chance to hit over the lake in front of the green to set up birdie. Classic risk-reward. Again, Outeniqua's par-4 18th (344 yards/316 metres) is a fun finish – the tee shot must carry over a lake with four bunkers down the left side of the fairway and another lake on the left side of the green and bunker guarding the right side.

Dine and wine

There are four restaurants to dine at. The award-winning La Cantina offers traditional Italian (including wood-fired pizza), Monet's at Fancourt, a restaurant and deli that has French cuisine (including chocolate eclairs) overlooking the Outeniqua course, the Club Lounge & Bar with American club food, and Henry White's for classic European cuisine.

One of my favorite things to do is to try local wines and Fancourt has partnered with three of Western Cape's vineyards (Graham Beck Wines, Jordan Wine Estate and Waterford Estate) so you can enjoy fine vintages with your food.

The accommodation

The Fancourt Hotel has 115 luxurious rooms and suites, all of which have a balcony to take in the mountain or Montagu course views. It starts at the Classic Room (344 square feet / 32 square metres) and moves through to the Two-Bedroom Suite (926 square feet / 86 square metres), which has its own dining area and fireplace. Each bedroom has its own bathroom.

The pro says: 'Montagu and Outeniqua, both sprawling parkland courses, are ranked number sixth and sixteenth in the country respectively, while Scottish links-inspired course The Links takes pride of place at number one.'
– Ryan Reid, Fancourt's Director of Sport & Recreation

The Manor House is a boutique lodging with 18 suites, each with butler-style service. Although it draws inspiration from the estate's original Blanco House, Manor features modern design and furnishing. Guests can enjoy the library, swimming pool, lounge for afternoon tea and bar.

Lodging starts with the Homewood Suite (60 square metres, 197 square feet), which has its own dining area, king bed, and balcony or patio. Or you can opt for the Master Bedroom (155 square metres, 508 square feet), two bedrooms with en suite bathrooms, and lounge and dining areas.

The Manor House won Africa's Best Romantic Boutique Hotel at the 2015 World Boutique Hotel Awards, so is a good option for couples.

Other activities

Younger guests might be attracted to the Kidz Club (for ages 3–10) or Teen Lounge with pool table, foosball and table tennis. Without a doubt, I'd be taking the family to explore the Garden Route area. Swim in the Indian Ocean at one of the local beaches or let Fancourt book you in for some horse riding, hiking and mountain biking. There are some highly-rated safari experiences nearby, too, such as the Gondwana Game Reserve, where lions, elephants, cheetahs and rhinos roam free. Wild times.

ABOVE: Fancourt Hotel Pool.

FLC Luxury Resort
Quy Nhon

Bình Định, Province, Vietnam

FLC Luxury Resort Quy Nhon

Location: Zone 4, Nhon Ly – Cat Tien Beach, Nhon Ly Commune, Binh Dinh Province, Vietnam

Website: flc.vn/en/du-an/flc-quy-nhon-beach-golf-resort

Phone number: 84 56 628 8888

If you are after an exotic luxury golfing vacation, then you should put FLC Luxury Resort Quy Nhon high on the list of destinations. This is more of a stay, play and chill-out-by-the-beach sojourn with daiquiri in hand than an adrenaline-filled getaway. Located on the golden coastline of mid-Vietnam, some 40 minutes by car from Phu Cat Airport, the resort is built around the beach and two golf courses as its central attractions.

FLC Quy Nhon Golf Links (the Ocean Course), the first to open in early 2016, was created by Nicklaus Design who laid the links-style course out over sand dunes, with ample views of Nhon Ly Beach and the South China Sea to enjoy. The Links won the award for Best New Course in Asia Pacific at the Asian Golf Awards 2016.

'The 18-hole golf course was built on natural sand with spectacular views of the sea from 14 different holes,' said Jim Wagner of Nicklaus Design. 'The front 9 is carved through an existing pine forest with a higher elevation than the back 9. The back 9 is routed along the sea and takes on a more rugged and playful character with large sand dunes helping to frame golf holes.'

The second course, the Mountain Course, was designed by fellow US company Schmidt and Curley (of Mission Hills fame). It offers more elevation changes and sits on higher ground above the resort with sweeping views of the sea on 16 of the 18 holes. This course opened only at the beginning of 2017 and was yet to have a slope and rating at time of publishing.

'We set out to create a course that was not just great itself, but also did its best to both compliment and contrast the existing Nicklaus-designed Ocean course on the property below us,' designer Brian Curley said. 'The Ocean course is wonderful and creates a character that makes the most of its tree-lined corridors and ocean-front dunes.

'On the Mountain Course, we chose to go in a slightly opposite direction, relying on width to accommodate the average player but still employing plenty of difficulty, especially at the greens, in order to keep the course challenging and fun.'

US construction company Flagstick, with the help of local labor, built both courses (it took just five and a half months to finish Links). Renowned Japanese golf writer Masa Nishijima rates FLC Quy Nhon as one of the top five resorts in Asia.

OPPOSITE: FLC Quy Nhon Golf Links.

The challenges

Links course: Miss the fairway and you'll be hitting off sand and straw, but there is minimal rough, and wide fairways should invite big hitters to let loose off most tees. Holes 6, 12 and 13 are challenging due to their length and difficulty around the greens. par or bogey is a great score if the wind picks up, especially on the par-4 hole 13, which plays straight at the sea.

The resort experience

FLC Quy Nhon Beach & Golf Resort is spread out over 741 acres (300 hectares) and makes full use of the views of Nhon Ly – Cat Tien Beach. As well as the two golf courses, it features a five-star hotel, luxury villas, a convention centre, pine forests and Hon Kho Island. The rooms feature contemporary décor and a mix of traditional and modern design. Watching the sun rise over the South China Sea to the east is not to be missed. There are outdoor and indoor swimming pools to cool off in, or you can lounge under an umbrella – you get the picture.

Type of grasses: Platinum TE Palspalum on greens, tees and fairways.

When to play: You can play year-round, although it rains regularly in the monsoon season from September to January and the hottest month is June, with an average temperature of 93° Fahrenheit (34° Celsius), according to Hikersbay.com.

Par: 72

Yardage: FLC Quy Nhon Golf Links – Ocean Course: 7,273 yards, 6,650 metres. Schmidt and Curley's Mountain Course: 7077 yards, 6471 metres

Slope: FLC Quy Nhon Golf Links: 133

Rating: FLC Quy Nhon Golf Links: 75.1

Best hole: On the Links course, the final three holes along the ocean and sand dunes are all superb.

The designer says: 'Although the par-4 13th will certainly leave a long-lasting impression on most golfers, the finishing sequence of holes 16–18 will be memorable for their endless sea views and the strategic impact of the stunning sand dunes that encompass parts of the last three holes.' – Jim Wagner, Nicklaus Design

Dine and wine

There are three restaurants to choose from: Mistral Top View, which is built on a hilly cove overlooking the Links course and ocean; Salsa the Beach Club covers most palates with Asian, Mediterranean, Brazilian BBQ and more common Western dishes; and Cheers Fun Pub encourages you to dance and eat tapas (but not at the same time). Elsewhere sip a daiquiri at Ocean Pool Bar or suck on a stogie at the Wine & Cigar Bar. Alternatively, opt for your own private meal as a chef cooks up a storm in your room.

The accommodation

There are 327 rooms and suites in total. Each of the 90 villas offers a higher level of privacy than the hotel rooms – so it might heighten the romance on this Vietnam getaway as you gaze out to the sea or take a dip in your swimming pool. Many villas have easy access to the beach, too. The villas feature modern interiors and range from two-bedroom suites (with king and double beds) with 2,347 square feet (218 square metres) to the four-bedroom Golf Villa (two king and two twin beds) with a luxurious 4,639 square feet (431 square metres). You won't have to go without satellite TV, A/C or high-speed internet either.

Other activities

It would be hard to go past The Spa. For a start, you could opt for ancient Cham purification rituals, which sounds quite liberating. There is also 'yogassage', herbal therapy and thalassa (or seawater) therapy. For those more adventurous types, head out on a kayak safari, explore the area on mountain bike, or take a boat trip to Hon Seo Island and snorkel over the coral reef near Rang Beach.

ABOVE: FLC Quy Nhon Golf Links.

ABOVE: Resort bar; *BELOW:* Resort Villa interior.

A view of the regal Gleneagles
Hotel from the King's Course.

Gleneagles Scotland

Gleneagles Scotland

Location: Auchterarder, Perthshire, PH3 1NF, Scotland
Website: www.gleneagles.com
Phone number: 44 01764 662231

It has a reputation as one of the leading golf resorts in Scotland, but Gleneagles offers a lot beyond the three championship courses on its property. It is one of the few resorts I've seen that features the aristocratic sport of falconry – it hosts the British School of Falconry – and that is just for starters for outdoor lovers who enjoy a taste of royal treatment on holidays. However, I'd gladly travel here for an epic golf trip. Approximately one hour's drive northwest from Edinburgh, you'll find a destination with three exceptional golf courses – the King's Course, the Queen's Course and the PGA Centenary Course – set in rich Scottish countryside. The nearby peaks of Ben Vorlich and Trossachs in the west, the rock-faced Grampian Mountains in the north and rolling hills in the south are a classic highland backdrop as you tee off, according to Canadian golf journalist Anita Draycott who has written highly about each layout.

The King's Club was designed by five-time Open Champion James Braid and opened in 1919 to challenge everyone from royalty to the best stroke makers in the game. Braid, one of the greats of Scottish golf, laid out a course that will test you from hole 1, 'Dun Whinny', with its giant bunker guarding a sloping green that drains into it, through to hole 18, 'King's Home', a 480-yard (439-metre) par 5 marked by a ridge line across the fairway, 10 bunkers and a green with severe undulations.

At less than 6,015 yards (5,500 metres), the Queen's Course – also the work of Braid – is short and feisty by comparison, according to Draycott. The moorland fairways wind their way between ridges and woodland in comparison to the more open King's Course. With its beauty, Queen's Course has enchanted everyone from pros Greg Norman and Tom Watson to the late great Scottish actor Sean Connery and astronaut Alan Shepard.

They would have been captivated by holes such as the 'Water Kelpie', the attractive par-3 hole 13, which has the Loch an Eerie on the right side and a bunker on the left of the green.

Finally, the PGA Centenary Course – formerly the Monarch's Course – was designed by Jack Nicklaus in the early 1990s and played host to the Ryders Cup in 2014, which was the first time a Scottish course had hosted the prestigious competition in 40 years. Europe retained the Cup that year, defeating the USA

OPPOSITE: King's Course.

16½ points to 11½ points. The PGA Centenary Course has also hosted the Scottish Open and Women's British Open.

There is also the nine-hole PGA National Academy Course and nine-hole Pitch and Putt to warm up on.

The challenges

Club selection for approach shots is the key to scoring at the King's Course, due to the stiff winds that whip over the hills. Slick greens and many well-placed bunkers are going to test even the best here. The Queen's Course challenges with elevation changes, trees that narrow tee shots, water hazards like a ploughman's ditch, dozens of bunkers and small or multi-level greens that can feature severe slopes and undulations. The PGA Centenary Course has the length to test today's top professionals who must navigate around water hazards, bunkers and tiered greens.

Type of grasses: The springy moorland turf is made up of a variety of grass mixes. The King's Course: Greens a mix of poa and bentgrass. Tees: poa and bentgrass. Fairways: poa, bentgrass, and fescue. Semi-rough: poa, bentgrass, ryegrass, and Fescue. The Queen's Course: Greens: poa and bentgrass. Tees: poa and bentgrass. Fairways: poa, bentgrass, and fescue. Semi-rough: poa, bentgrass, fescue, and ryegrass. PGA Centenary Course: Greens: poa and bentgrass. Tees: poa and bentgrass. Fairways: poa, bentgrass, and fescues. Semi-rough: fescue.

When to play: The course is open all year subject to weather and maintenance, however,

December through to February will have chilly conditions with average temperatures sitting between 43° and 46° Fahrenheit (6° and 8° Celsius).

Par: King's Course 71; Queen's Course 70; The PGA Centenary Course 72

Yardage: King's Course 6,790 yards, 6,209 metres; Queen's Course 5,965 yards, 5,454 metres; The PGA Centenary Course 7,296 yards, 6,671 metres.

Slope: King' Course 139 *; Queen's Course N/A; The PGA Centenary Course 145

Rating: King' Course N/A; Queen's Course N/A ; The PGA Centenary Course 77

The resort experience

The Gleneagles Hotel is a regal-looking chateau that started operating in 1924, after being built by the Caledonian Railway Company. It currently offers 232 rooms, including 26 luxury suites. This is a Five-Red-Star property – the highest service rating in the United Kingdom.

What is especially attractive about Gleneagles is that you have unlimited use of the Club for the price of your room. That includes a huge array of facilities (including the Alpen Onsen hot pool and sauna) complimentary activities (including fitness classes such as yoga and Tai Chi, lawn croquet, pitch and putt, and tennis).

Dine and wine

You can expect to be treated like royalty in any of the resort's four restaurants. Gleneagles' chef Andrew Fairlie has earned two Michelin Stars for the restaurant that bears his name. Try the degustation menu, a nine-course festival for the taste buds that starts with ballotine of foie gras, peach and almond milk and ends with coffee and chocolates. Fairlie uses herbs, vegetables, salads and fruit from their own walled Victorian garden. Fine wines are sourced from boutique vineyards as far as Tasmania and matched with each course.

You'll also find Scottish/French dishes at The Stathearn, Mediterranean fare at Deseo, and an all-day menu at the Dormy Clubhouse Bar and Grill. You might enjoy a tipple at one of three bars, or cup of tea or coffee in two lounges.

The accommodation

There is no cookie-cutter approach to the rooms here – each room has a unique layout. Everything from an Estate Room with views of the Perthshire countryside

ABOVE: Vitality Pool; *OPPOSITE:* Hotel room interior.

through to family rooms that can accommodate up to two little people is available. There are two basic interior styles throughout to choose: Modern or traditional.

Other activities

As previously mentioned, there is an interesting array of aristocratic activities for lovers of the outdoors. You can choose target shooting, falconry, indoor/outdoor tennis, wildlife photography, equestrian school, road cycling or dog training amongst others, but you'll find me with a fly-fishing rod and a dry fly on the end of it, trying to fool a trout in one of the lochs. A ESPA spa and wellness centre with vitality pool,hair salon and nail bar round out the magnificent selection.

* Source: www.scotlandgolf.com/scotlandgolfcourses/t-z/thegleneagleshotelgolfcourses.html

Best hole: King's Course: You'll enjoy Hole 13 – 'Braids Brawest' or in other words, designer James Braid's best. The 464-yard (424-metre) par 4 challenges with fairway undulations and the Auld Nick fairway bunker on the left, all with the pretty Ochil Hills in the background. Land your approach past the pin for an uphill putt.

Queen's Course: 'Queen's Hame', the picturesque par-4 hole 18, sees you hitting from an elevated tee over a small loch called the 'Deuk Dubs', before trying to land the approach on the right level of the two-tier green for the flag position. Golf course manager Scott Fenwick loves 'Drum Sichy',

the par-4 Hole 6, with an elevated green that is framed by bunkers.

PGA Centenary Course: Hole 4 'Gowden Bestie', a classic Nicklaus challenge, has 239 yards (219 metres) before you reach a green that is guarded by a giant bunker on the left. The green rises to a plateau before falling away at the back. Also brilliant is the redesigned 18th, a par 5 dubbed 'Dun Roamin' that gives big hitters a chance at eagle on the 533-yard (487 metre) hole.

The designer says: 'It's the finest parcel of land in the world I have ever been given to work with.'
– Jack Nicklaus on the PGA Centenary Course

Gokarna Forest Resort Course features narrow fairways, elevated tees and large greens.

Gokarna
Forest Resort

Kathmandu, Nepal

Gokarna Forest Resort

Location: Rajnikunj, Thali – 7, Kageswari, Manahara, Kathmandu, Nepal
Website: www.gokarna.com
Phone number: 977 1 445 1212

Gokarna Forest Resort is tucked away in the Gokarna Protected Forest, a preserve that was once a private royal hunting ground for the Kings of Nepal. They didn't have to venture too far from the palace for some sport. Gokarna is a beautiful spot considering it is just over 6 miles (10 kilometres) to the city of Kathmandu and an even shorter distance to the Tribhuvan International Airport.

Nepal is a country that surprises because of the warmth of its people as much as the striking beauty of its Himalayan mountain range, which draws so many visitors each year. But golf is not the first thing that comes to mind when you think about Nepal, although I have had a memorable round at altitude there. Gokarna Forest Resort's championship 18-hole course shows that could soon be changing. This 6,750-yard (6,172-metre) layout was designed by David McLay Kidd, a Scottish architect who grew up playing some of the oldest courses in the game and who got his break designing Oregon's brilliant Bandon Dunes links. As well as being the top ranked course in Nepal by Top100GolfCourses.com in 2017, Gokarna is now considered one of South Asia's finest courses.

The undulating fairways have been carved inside a forest that stretches for some 470 acres (190 hectares), and they pass streams and inbetween hills as they progress through what once was a forbidden valley. The view from the 1st tee has the 21,969-foot (6,696-metre) Mount Dorjee Lakpa standing majestically in front of you. In classic Himalayan fashion, tees are often elevated and as high up as 197-feet (60 metres) on hillsides, according to Deepak Acharya, Senior Golf Director of Gokarna Forest Resort. Acharya considers the fairways to be narrow in comparison to the 'huge' greens.

'Designer David McLay Kidd has marvelously crafted variations with the outlook of each hole,' he said. 'The majority of visitors want to play the course a number of times. Long and straight hitters have the advantage on the golf course.'

Watch out for the cheeky monkeys, flying foxes, spotted deer as you progress through the forest. I can't wait to play here.

The challenges

It is not the longest course, but narrow fairways put a premium on accuracy. The pro's tips: 'Try to avoid the jungle. On most parts of the front nine, keep to the left

OPPOSITE: Gokarna Forest Resort Course.

side of the fairway, and on the back nine avoid the stream that runs all along the back nine. Since the greens are really big in size, practise putting before starting to understand the pace of the green.'

The resort experience

The Nepalase are some of the friendliest people you'll meet and you can expect the guest service here to be just as special. Gokarna is a forest retreat with a mix of classic resort features, including a spa with a variety of massages (the focus is on ancient holistic Ayurvedic treatments), a gym and health club with personal trainers, and a heated indoor pool, jacuzzi and sauna. The Malla- and Rana-period architecture suits the jungle-forest setting. Have a sun session on one of the courtyard chairs and soak in the mountain views. The morning yoga sounds like a smart way to limber up for golf, too. There is a free shuttle from the airport to get you here.

Type of grasses: The fairway has a mixture of Tifdwarf Bermuda and local cow grass, whereas the greens are a mixture of putter, A4 and L93 bentgrasses.

When to play: The golf course is open 365 days a year.

Par: 72

Yardage: 6,755 yards, 6,140 metres

Slope: 119

Rating: 71.5

Best hole: The par-3 hole 8 is the signature hole and a daunting challenge. It plays 225 yards (206 metres) from the back tees and some 20–25 yards longer when the pin is at the back. There is trouble on the left side, and a deep pot-hole bunker guards the crest-shaped green on the right. The average score during professional tournaments was 3.8 in 2016.

The pro says: 'The forest, majestic views, undulating fairways, perfect rolls on the greens, and wildlife on the course – monkeys and deer – are the biggest attractions. And Kathmandu's weather, between 20–30° Centigrade during the day throughout the year, is icing on the cake.' –Deepak Acharya, Senior Golf Director

Dine and wine

There are four different eateries. The Hunter's Lodge Restaurant serves Nepali specialties, Durbar Restaurant (or King's Palace) has international fare and the Club House Restaurant features Chinese and Thai dishes. In the evening, sip on a glass of champagne at the 8848 Mt Bar, which also features live music. Breakfast is included with the rooms.

The accommodation

The rooms feature modern interiors, polished floorboards or tiled floors, and elegant décor. Nepali art adds to the exotic feel and there are views of the course and mountains. There are six different options, starting with the Cottage Room (344–377 square feet, 32–35 square metres), which comes with herbal bath amenities, two bottles of water (always drink purified water in Nepal) and morning yoga. At the other end of the scale, the Gokarna Suite (1,001 square feet, 93 square metres) is a duplex with one or two open-planned bedroom and square bath tubs.

Other activities

What better way to explore Gokarna Protected Forest than on horseback? The resort's stable has a variety of horses and ponies that should work for riders of all experience levels. You can also hire a bicycle, take part in jungle paint ball, go bird watching or head out for a one-to-four-hour guided forest walk.

ABOVE: Gokarna Forest Resort Course.

OPPOSITE TOP: Courtyard Garden; *MIDDLE:* Swimming Pool; *BOTTOM:* Tower Suite.

The Old White Course – Hole No. 14.

The Greenbrier

West Virginia, United States

The Greenbrier

Location: 300 W Main St, White Sulphur Springs, West Virginia 24986, United States
Website: www.greenbrier.com
Phone number: 1 855 453 4858

Sitting in a valley in the beautiful Allegheny Mountains in the small West Virginian city of White Sulphur Springs, The Greenbrier is one of the oldest and most prestigious golf resorts in the United States. It features five championship golf courses by American designers, including the Old White TPC, The Greenbrier, The Meadows, The Snead and Oakhurst Links, the oldest golf club in America, having opened in 1884. The first three are open to resort guests who get a discount over members of the public.

In 2016, severe flooding caused extensive damage to the golf courses, especially Old White TPC, The Snead and The Meadows. But it wasn't just the golf courses impacted by the deadly flood, as *Golf Digest*'s Tim Rosafort reported. 'Greenbrier owner Jim Justice reached out to people who lost their loved ones and homes and had no place to go. He opened the doors of his resort to feed and house the displaced. More than 200 took him up on the invitation, some among the resort's 1,800 employees who live in the area.'

The staff at the famous resort and White Sulphur Springs residents were quick to start rebuilding. The Old White TPC is a 1914 Charles Blair Macdonald design and the restoration work that was done to modernize and fix this famous course tried to remain as true to the pioneering American architect's original concept as possible, according to Jamie Hamilton, Greenbrier's Associate Director of Golf.

'All of the work we've done during its restoration was done with the intent of honoring and showing his hole templates, features and design elements in the most authentic way possible.'

The Old White TPC is the host course for the PGA TOUR's Greenbrier Classic and is the only Macdonald design available to the public in the US. This is one course to play and tick off the bucket list.

'It is the perfect combination of traditional design, over 100 years of history, modern tournament experience and a brand-new restoration featuring new grass types across the course,' said Hamilton.

Since the flood, The Meadows has had significant routing changes from Dick Wilson's 1963 layout and other major renovations including the introduction of riveted bunkers throughout the course.

'As the only course on property, and one of relatively few in the US to feature this

Type of grasses: The Old White TPC has T-1 Bentgrass fairways and V8 Bentgrass greens. The Meadows has T-1 Bentgrass fairways and 007 Bentgrass greens. The Greenbrier's grasses are to be determined.

When to play: The Old White TPC's season is generally April through to November, while The Meadows is March through to December. The Greenbrier's best months are April through to October considering its position along the mountains. The winter months of January and February are generally too chilly for golf.

Par: The Old White TPC: 70. The Meadows: 70

Yardage: The Old White TPC: approx. 7,300 yards, or 6,675 metres. The Meadows: approx. 6,600 yards, or 6,035 metres.

Best hole: The Old White TPC's hole 18 is a 175-yard (160-metre) par 3 dubbed 'Home'. It has been the site of high drama at the finish of The Greenbrier Classic with play at the final green regularly deciding the winner, often during playoffs. The Meadows new hole 16 will likely be the signature hole, with a large drop in elevation and some lovely mountain views on the dogleg-left par 4. The Greenbrier's tough 456-yard (417-metre) hole 6 is one to watch out for, too.

design element, we knew it would provide our golfers with a memorable and unique experience,' said Hamilton.

'The Meadows will impress golfers as a dramatically improved version that utilizes some of our best creek-side land, mountain vistas, newly-introduced riveted bunkers along with updated greens and grass across the property.'

The Greenbrier was designed by American Seth Raynor in 1924 and renovated by Jack Nicklaus in 1978 before it hosted the Ryder Cup the following year (the US team won). The heavily-wooded course also hosted the Solheim Cup in 1994 (the US won again). There are some challenging holes here including the 456-yard (417-metre) hole 6 with its narrow fairway and green that is protected by a huge bunker. It didn't stop Sam Snead shooting 59 in the final round of the 1959 Spring Festival, the first to achieve this score in competition. The Greenbrier is set to be renovated again under the guidance of Phil Mickelson in 2017.

The Snead, a Tom Fazio course that opened in 2004, is open only to members and there are limited tee times for non-members at Oakhurst Links, which is a more recent addition to the Greenbrier Resort. Modern golf sticks are not allowed here – instead players hit gutta-percha balls with hickory shafted sticks.

ABOVE: Greenbrier Golf Course; *OPPOSITE:* The Greenbrier's front entrance.

The challenges

On the Old White TPC you'll face many risk-reward holes and it is about weighing up whether it is worth going for the green or laying up, especially with the number of bunkers protecting greens. 'Macdonald liked to give players two options on most shots – the safe shot to the larger part of the fairway/green and the bold line where trouble comes into play,' said Greenbrier pro Jamie Hamilton. 'As golfers play the course, they have to decide on a shot-by-shot basis whether the risk is worth the reward or if the safer play is the better option.'

'On The Meadows, the key will be keeping it in the fairway off the tee as there are many tight driving holes. If a player can keep it in the fairway and avoid the green-side bunkers, it is a relatively short course and they can score well.'

The resort experience

Golf is the central focus of the Greenbrier, a regular stop on the PGA Tour that has rich sporting history and three championship courses open for visitors. However, the

The pro says: 'The Old White TPC is the only Charles Blair Macdonald golf course available to the public and is an outstanding example of his highly-regarded design style. Additionally, as the host course for the PGA Tour's Greenbrier Classic, it plays host to some of the best golfers in the world every summer.

The Meadows will impress golfers as a dramatically improved version that utilizes some of our best creek-side land, mountain vistas, newly introduced riveted bunkers along with updated greens and grass across the property.' – Jamie Hamilton, Associate Director of Golf

Greenbrier started welcoming guests in 1778, well before the game we love flourished in North America. Instead, people were drawn to the natural mineral springs that were found at the 11,000-acre (4,452-hectare) property – the same sulphur spring water is used today in the Mineral Spa for hydrotherapy and bathing.

There is a great sense of tradition at this resort – the Greenbrier is a National Historic Landmark. The hotel is an enormous grand white building whose famous façade and pillars are reminiscent of the White House. Pioneering interior designer Dorothy Draper directed the renovation of the luxury hotel after it was used as a hospital during World War II.

There are 33 suites, 710 rooms and 96 cottages and the interiors have a colorful and homey look to them. The resort boasts that 26 of the 45 US Presidents have stayed at the Greenbrier. It wasn't just golf that these leaders enjoyed here – there are more than 55 activities at the resort as well as plenty of fine dining. The luxury holiday destination has continued to receive awards and plaudits for its services, such as being included in *Condé Nast Traveler*'s *Gold List: The World's Best Places to Stay* in 2014 and *Travel + Leisure*'s *Top Resorts in the Continental US* in 2014.

Dine and wine

The Greenbrier features 20 restaurants, cafes, and lounges so it will take a long stay to try each of them. A team of 12 chefs, along with three sommeliers to match fine wines, are behind these culinary experiences. The Main Dining Room has been serving guests since 1913. You can enjoy a buffet breakfast there or maybe have a coffee and pastry at The Greenbrier Gourmet. Sam Snead's at the Golf Club (soups, salads, wood-fired pizza) and Slammin' Sammy's (burgers) pay homage to the legendary golfer who was the professional at The Greenbrier. You can head to one of these restaurants during the golf season for lunch. In-Fusion's menu covers Chinese, Japanese and Thai, and it also sits next to the casino for those who enjoy a flutter on the roulette or blackjack tables. I favor a medium-grilled steak at Prime 44 West instead.

The accommodation

Signature Resort Rooms, Legacy Cottages (two to four bedrooms), Greenbrier Estate Homes (four to seven bedrooms) and the Windsor Club (one- to seven-bedroom suites) are available. The Dorothy Draper décor and interiors are colorful and traditional in keeping with the historic resort. Starting at a Gable Room (150 square feet, 14 square metres) with a double bed and flat-screen TV, and going all the way through to the seven-bedroom Presidential Suite, there are plenty of choices here. We assume the presidents chose the latter option, which has a library, a living room with grand piano, dining room, and patio across two floors. All the secret service agents could get a king-size bed (if they're allowed to sleep).

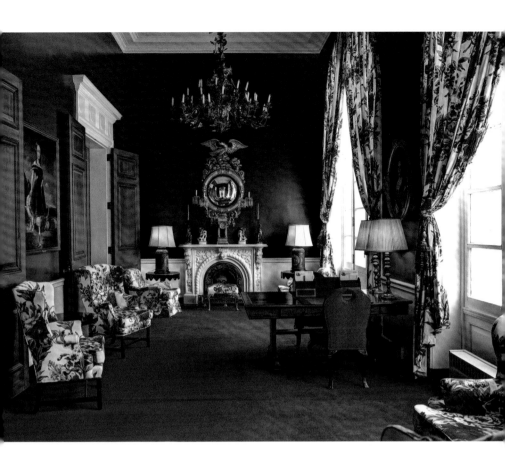

Other activities

Perhaps the most surprising thing about The Greenbrier is the number of activities available on the 11,000-acre (4,450-hectare) property. The resort boasts over 55 of them, some being seasonal, such as shooting ringneck pheasants. My favorites are the canopy tour (seven ziplines and five cable bridges plus rappelling), guided fly-fishing for trout in Second Creek (all gear provided), swimming in the Olympic-size indoor pool or heated infinity outdoor pool, movies at the cinema, and the Adventure Zone for kids, which has everything from bowling to horse-riding. I'll also be taking the history tour of the declassified bunker at The Greenbrier. It's no wonder so many presidents came to play golf here – they wanted to check out the emergency Cold War fall-out shelter, which is carved deep inside a mountain beneath the West Virginia Wing of the resort. This is a golf resort with a difference.

ABOVE: Victorian Writing Room.

Hualalai Golf Course – the fairway is laid out between jagged lava rock on Hole No. 7.

Hualalai
– Four Seasons

Hualalai – Four Seasons

Location: 72–100 Kaupulehu Dr, Kailua-Kona, Island of Hawaii, USA
Website: www.fourseasons.com/hualalai
Phone number: 1 808 325 8000

There are some superb resort courses on the island of Hawaii including Mauna Kea and Hapuna, where you can play next to the Pacific Ocean in tropical conditions. Four Seasons Hualalai is another wonderful resort that offers exceptional luxury accommodation and top-shelf golf.

Hualalai is a links-style course designed by Jack 'The Golden Bear' Nicklaus and opened in 1996 next to the luxury Four Seasons resort. The unusual feature here: Its groomed fairways have been laid between lava flows that have cooled down to a jagged black rock. You don't want to go looking for your ball in there as your shoes will barely survive. The contrast between the green fairways and black lava that stands like walls on either side of the fairway is stunning. There are unsighted shots over these ancient lava flows. On the 7th, the lava makes a narrow canyon in the middle of the fairway – one of the most unusual hazards I've seen on a golf course.

Hualalai hosts the PGA Champions Tour each January and it has the facilities to match that occasion. Even so, the course is designed to be forgiving for casual golfers.

The 18th has a stunning outlook of Waiakauhi Beach. You'd never know that the resort was damaged by the tsunami of March 2011, after an earthquake off the coast of Japan sent a massive tidal wave across the Pacific. It ploughed into the waterfront suites and lifted a deck onto the middle of the fairway.

The challenges
Apart from some unsighted shots over the lava flows, there are some long, well-placed fairway bunkers to contend with. However, the fairways generally offer wide landing areas off the tee.

The resort experience
Four Seasons Hualalai offers your classic beach-side vacation. There are many areas to chill out or get wet. There are seven swimming areas in total – including the adults-only Palm Grove pool with swim-up bar, and the King's Pond, a 1.8-million gallon (6.8-million litre) salt-water aquarium carved out of lava

OPPOSITE: Golf Course from above.

and stocked full of marine life. Here you can snorkel with some 4,000 tropical fish from more than 98 species, including a spotted eagle ray.

Unwind at the 28,000-square-foot (2,600-square-metre) Hualalai Spa, which has a stream running through the tropical garden as well as saunas, steam rooms, soaking tubs and cold plunges. Body treatments include massages such as a hau'oli wawae, which takes care of the foot, neck and scalp, and coffee mocha scrub (coffee-infused salt).

Beach weddings take place in the tropical space here, and honeymoons for that matter, too. And with children 12 and under playing golf for free when accompanied by a paying guest, they are keeping families in mind, too.

Dine and wine

There are three ocean-side restaurants and two lounges. There's al fresco dining at Beach Tree during the day, or get stuck into the fresh sushi at 'Ulu Lounge or

---

Type of grasses: The Tifdwarf Bermuda greens are quick and firm like a pool table but reasonably easy to read. Fairways of Tifway II Bermuda grass.

When to play: Year-round.

Yardage: 7,117 yards; 6,507 metres

Slope: 139

Rating: 73.7

Best hole: I'll go with the picturesque par-3 17th, which has the ocean crashing into the lava on the left and a giant bunker in front of the green. I played a pitching wedge off the lava (note, not good for clubs).

The pro says: 'The 17th tee – my favorite part of my office. This little hole is spectacular... Jack [Nicholas] has taken this black lava, the white sand, the blue ocean and sky, and the green grass and contrasted it in a very dramatic way. It is a nice little par 3 as long as you keep in mind the wind... Aim to the left side of the green or even the left rocks.' – Brendan Moynahan, Director of Golf Operations * taste a Mahi Mahi at Hualalai Grille. At night, enjoy a drink next to the firepit at the 'Ulu Ocean Grill restaurant. You can even organize a private luau at the Hoku Amphitheater with that special someone. Hula and fire dancers put on a show while you feast on a five-course meal.

The accommodation

Hualalai has 51 suites and villas and 125 guest rooms, each with lava-rock garden showers. This is luxurious accommodation with a truly Hawaiian touch. You can choose something as big as a three-bedroom Makaloa Villa, which is more like a private beach home and has its own pool and whirlpool. The Oceanfront Room can comfortably fit two adults and a child and gives you a superb view of the Pacific Ocean.

Other activities

There are plenty of ocean adventures to enjoy, such as a ribcraft snorkelling tour, whale-watching, stand-up paddle boarding or paddling a four-man outrigger canoe. There are scores of activities here for all the family to enjoy, too, from basketball and tennis to Hawaiian crafts and sand sculpting. Or learn how to make a flower lei – the aroma is delightful.

*Source: www.fourseasons.com/hualalai

ABOVE: Resort Pool.

OPPOSITE ABOVE: Resort Exterior; *LEFT:* Bathroom Interior; *RIGHT:* Hualalai Golf Course.

Tricky greens ... the Iberostar Playa Paraíso Golf Course.

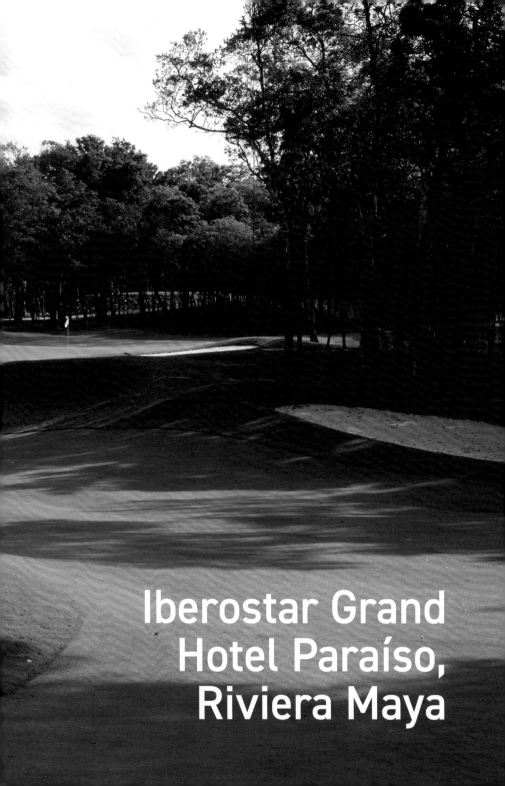

Iberostar Grand
Hotel Paraíso,
Riviera Maya

Quintana Roo, Mexico

Iberostar Grand Hotel Paraíso, Riviera Maya

Location: Carretera Chetumal – P. Juarez Km. 309, Playa Paraiso, 77710 Playa del Carmen, Q.R., Mexico
Website: www.iberostar.com/en/hotels/riviera-maya/iberostar-grand-paraiso
Phone number: 888 923 2722

I can just picture it – somewhere beautiful to relax in the sun. Somewhere south of the border, down Mexico way. The Grand Hotel Paraíso will do just fine. This impressive resort is located on the Riveria Maya, on the Caribbean coastline of north-east Yucatán Peninsula. We're talking gorgeous turquoise waters and tropical conditions in and out of the water. But before you grab a daiquiri and a hammock, you'll want to play the championship golf course. It was designed by P.B. Dye, the youngest son of renowned American course architect Peter Dye. He has picked up some techniques from his father in terms of challenging golfers with smart layout and visual trickery. Greg Bond, the director of golf at the Iberostar Playa Paraíso Golf Club, sums up the challenges of the undulating course this way: 'Extreme vertical movement, treacherously sloping greens, beautiful hand-laid stone work with an authentic Mayan touch and perfect playing conditions,' Bond said. 'P.B. Dye set out to create a golf course that is visually intimidating. Although many of the holes seem tighter than a bowling alley, the reality is there is more room than meets the eye.'

The course works its way through jungle vegetation. Some eye-catching stonework pays tribute to the ancient Mayan civilization as you work your ball down the fairways. At the end of the 9th hole, there's even a replica El Castillo pyramid from the Chichén Itzá Mayan ruins (which are located about two hours' drive inland). Extreme elevation changes, deep bunkers, blind shots and tight fairways keep things interesting on this golf course.

'What this fun P.B. Dye course lacks in gulf views it makes up for with huge undulations – in its fairways and its greens – and tons of visual variety,' *Golf Digest's* Peter Finch wrote after touring the area. 'It's definitely worth buying a yardage book here because the course holds many mysteries for first-timers.'

I never like playing on an empty stomach. Fortunately, the package you book into at Iberostar means that you can have your fill of food and drinks before, during or after your round. US golf writer Bob Fagan rates this as the best 'all-inclusive' hotel and golf course combination he has experienced in his wide travels.

OPPOSITE: Iberostar Playa Paraíso Golf Course.

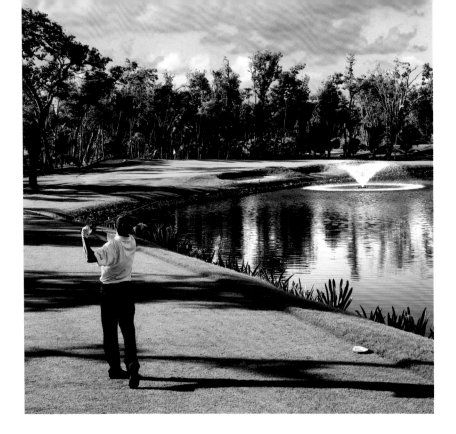

Iberostar Playa Paraíso has hosted the *Big Break Mexico* Golf Channel competition as well as the Canadian Tour events and the 2016 World Amateur Team Championships.

The challenges

Hit it straight, trust the yardage book and bring your best putting game on these sloping, tiered greens.

Type of grasses: Paspalum Sea Isle 2000 greens and Paspalum Sea Isle 1 fairways, tees and rough.

When to play: The course is open 365 days a year in the tropical conditions.

Par: 72

Yardage: 6,704 yards, 6,034 metres

Slope: 137

Rating: 74.3

Best hole: The 427-yard par-4 9th is the signature hole. You'll be hitting over a rock river bed off the tee, with a fairway bunker on the left and two on the right.

The pro says: 'This course challenges every part of your game; it is absolutely one of the best true tests of golf I've seen anywhere. You must be a complete player to play well here. Additionally, the course conditions compete with any facility in the US, Canada or Mexico.' – Greg Bond, Director of Golf

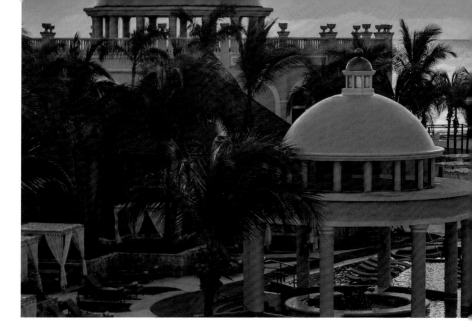

The resort experience

Iberostar Grand Hotel Paraiso is a four-diamond, five-star, adults-only resort about 30 minutes' drive south from Cancun International Airport. Ornate and elaborate, the hotel is built in a Neo-Renaissance style and features marble floors, large columns, interior gardens and a ceiling painting on the interior of a dome.

Being 'all-inclusive', guests can enjoy their food and drinks at the restaurants, the minibar, or use the 24-hour room service as part of the package price. You can start to relax as soon as you arrive at the hotel and someone hands you a glass of champagne at check-in. When you've finished unpacking, a concierge will hand you a towel, sun-screen and a newspaper to read poolside.

There are in fact three pools – one with sea water and an aqua-bar, a heated indoor pool and another with fine views. A white-sand beach is right out the front, where you can sit on a pool chair and doze off between swims. A butler service is also ready to shine your shoes back at the hotel. Resort activities are also included for the one price and there are dozens to help you burn off all unwanted calories.

Dine and wine

Get ready to eat and eat well. There are four *a la carte* restaurants, a 5-star Bella Vista buffet, five bars and 24-hour room service, featuring a wide variety of meals and drinks. You can choose Venezia Italian Restaurant, teppanyaki Japanese at Haiku (catch the food on your plate after chef cooks it in front of you), authentic Mexican dishes at La Brisa and Toni's Surf and Turf fare. Iberostar push their chefs to create new menus as seen by Chef On Tour, an initiative that showcases the creativity of the group's Michelin-star chefs. I might put on some weight here.

The accommodation

The Grand Hotel Paraíso has 10 accommodation options all with concierge and butler service and a customizable mini-bar. It's not a small development – this includes 300 Grand Suites overlooking the ocean or gardens, 10 secluded villas and two Presidential Suites. Even a basic suite comes with a balcony and views. Use the pillow menu to get the right fit for your king-size or queen-size bed. The marble bathrooms feature double-vanity sinks and a whirlpool bath. Satellite TV channels and a DVD player are also standard. You get a separate dining room, wrap-around terrace and a hammock with the Presidential Suite.

Other activities

The activities, which are included in the package, take this resort to another level. There is a focus on fitness here – which works well after the buffet. The fitness centre has yoga, TRX, tai chi, spinning sessions, kick boxing and aerobics. Outside you can enjoy archery, tennis, basketball, volleyball, beach volleyball and shooting. In the water, take a catamaran or kayak out for a spin, try snorkeling in the Caribbean Sea, get a taste of scuba diving in the pool, or play water polo. You'll have to pay extra for the jet-skiing, sailing lessons, water skiing, parasailing, winding surfing and PADI diving school course, but I'm not sure you'll have time for all of these.

After all that, you've earned a Thai massage at Spa Sensations, which has a sauna, Roman and Turkish baths, thalassotherapy (seawater) pools and a Mayan-style Temazcal (sweat lodge).

ABOVE: Main hotel pool.

The Pines Course Hole No. 6
at Sanctuary Cove.

InterContinental
Sanctuary Cove

InterContinental Sanctuary Cove

Location: Manor Cir, Sanctuary Cove, Queensland, 4212, Australia
Website: www.intercontinentalsanctuarycove.com
Phone number: 61 7 5530 1234

Situated just north of Queensland's famous Gold Coast, Sanctuary Cove is a prime destination for vacationing golfers Down Under. The InterContinental Resort is nestled next to two championship golf courses – The Pines and The Palms. The Pines is Australia's only Arnold Palmer signature course. The 7,197-yard (6,581-metre) layout is carved into 250 acres (101 hectares) of pine forest, with golfers given narrow fairway corridors on several holes. 14 of the holes are shaped around six man-made lakes. It's likely you'll run across a kangaroo or two as you progress around the course as well as plenty of birdlife, such as ducks, pelicans and kookaburras.

You are straight into the forest on the 1st hole, a 406-yard (371-metre) par 4 that has a line of tall trees that ensure you must control your drive through before attacking a green with three bunkers surrounding it. On hole 13, you'll be hitting across a lake on the 220-yard (201-metre) par 3, which has four bunkers protecting the green.

'What takes the golfer at first is the sheer beauty of the towering pines framing most holes, and the picturesque pine straw at their bases,' said golf professional Matt Ballard. 'That combination makes for some spectacular and intimidating tee shots. Again, these reflect Palmer's aggressive style in that golfers are invited to take risky lines, only to get to the ball and realize the rough cuts in and out of the fairway edges.'

The Pines course was ranked No. 45 in the country in 2016 by *Australian Golf Digest*. The Palms Course was considered a much lesser layout until it was redesigned by Australian architect Ross Watson and reopened in April 2011. It was a complete overhaul of the original design, re-routing the layout and reshaping and regrassing the greens. It jumped up the *Australian Golf Digest* rankings to 48 in 2016. The fairways wind between cabbage palms, and you'll face plenty of water hazards and deep bunkers that protect undulating greens. It is shorter than The Pines at 6,456 yards (5,903 metres) but will still challenge golfers of all standards with holes such as the 314-yard (287-metre) hole 3, a par 4 that has a lake on the right side of the fairway and a giant bunker on the left.

OPPOSITE: Palms course.

If that is not enough, Sanctuary Cove guests are invited to try the nearby Links Hope Island course, which was designed by five-times British Open champion Peter Thomson.

The challenges

The Pines offers some narrow corridors to hit through, tricky bunkering and 14 holes wrapped around lakes. The Palms is the easier course, with more open tee shots and wider fairways.

The resort experience

InterContinental Sanctuary Cove Resort has become a popular spot for businesses having conferences and individuals looking for a place to relax not too far from the

When to play: Queensland's sunny coastline is the ideal climate for golf, year-round.

Par: The Pines 72. The Palms 70

Yardage: The Pines 7,197 yards, 6,581 metres The Palms 6,456 yards, 5,904 metres

Slope: The Pines 132. The Palms 130

Rating: The Pines 74. The Palms 72

Best hole: The Pines' par-5 3rd hole is a 516-yard (472-metre) dogleg left with four fairway bunkers down the left side and three on the right side. It will take two accurate shots to make the green in two. The signature hole on the Palms is the par-3 hole 16. It may only be 160 yards (146 metres) to the green but you'll have to carry over water all the way and avoid the deep bunkering around the putting surface.

The pro says: 'Don't try to overpower both The Pines and Palms golf courses. If the tall pines don't get you, the water hazards will... The Palms is a lot more forgiving than The Pines – at least from tee to green. Tee shots are far more open, with wider fairways, and rough populated by palm trees that offer less challenging escapes.' – Matt Ballard golden beaches of the Gold Coast. The luxury hotel offers 243 rooms and suites in a variety of buildings spread out across a leafy property next to the Coomera River and Sanctuary Cove village.

The concierge will transfer you to the golf courses by buggy and organize sunscreen, lunch or clubs. As well as access to the Sanctuary Cove Country Club (with gym, 25-metre heated pool, tennis courts, spa, sauna, and fitness classes) and Sanctuary Cove Golf Club, you can book yourself for a treatment at the Champions Hair Beauty Day Spa. The highlight that I remember from Sanctuary Cove is the one-acre salt-water lagoon pool with sandy-beach. It's a great place to relax. There's even a chapel for celebrating weddings at the resort.

Dine and wine

Resort guests can choose between four dining venues. The Fireplace is Sanctuary Cove's signature restaurant. Head chef Matt Hart is behind a kitchen that has garnered praise for its steaks, wood-fired cuisine, and wine selection (it received 2 Wine Glasses from *Gourmet Traveller Wine* in 2016). The menu is seasonal, with the produce sourced locally. You can also get a buffet breakfast at Cove Café, sip on a cocktail or enjoy a light appetizer at The Pool House by the terrace pool, or have a chilled Australian beer at the Verandah Bar.

The accommodation

The Great House is the main hub, with the lobby, three restaurants and the spa. There are seven lodging options in different buildings throughout the property each with light interiors and modern décor. They range from a Classic Room (37 square

ABOVE: Fountain terrace.
OPPOSITE LEFT: Federation Lounge room; *RIGHT:* Federation bedroom; *BELOW:* Lagoon pool.

metre, 398 square foot) to a more luxurious Manor Suite with balconies, a lounge room (with fire place), kitchen, board room and jacuzzi.

Other activities

On the water, head out from the marina for some deep-sea fishing on a charter boat. It's possible to spot a humpback whale between July and November when they are migrating. The Gold Coast is famous for its theme parks. Dreamworld, Warner Bros. Movie World, Sea World and Wet'N'Wild are fun for the entire family.

Back at the resort, you'll find a games room with foosball, table tennis and board and card games. For outside fun, there's a giant chess set, cricket sets (nothing like backyard cricket in summer, folks) and bocce. And Planet Trekkers is a kids' club with a variety of supervised activities for youngsters in two blocks – to give mum and dad a break.

The ITC Grand Bharat and The
Classic Golf & Country Club.

ITC
Grand Bharat,
Gurugram

ITC Grand Bharat, Gurugram

Location: Bissar Akbarpur, Haryana 122102, India
Website: www.itchotels.com/in/en/itcgrandbharat-gurugram/leisure-recreation/golf
Phone number: 91 1267 285500

You'll find ITC Grand Bharat after a little over an hour's drive south-west of New Delhi's Indira Gandhi International Airport in north India. The luxury retreat sits on a 3,000-acre (1,214-hectare) estate in the Aravali Hills and it features a 27-hole complex designed by Jack Nicklaus, the Golden Bear's first signature course in South Asia. Before you hit a ball, the grand Indian architecture of the hotel's main building and apartment complex will strike you. The pale, ornate buildings are set against lush manicured grounds and the golf courses. It made an impression on Canadian golf writer Dave Finn when he visited. He described it as an 'oasis of tranquility.'

'The ITC Grand Bharat is maybe the most opulent hotel you will find anywhere in India.'

It is interesting to note that India was one of the first countries to embrace golf after the United Kingdom. The Royal Calcutta Golf Club was founded in 1829 and claims to be the oldest golf club outside of Britain. The All-India Amateur Championship had its inaugural event there in 1892. ITC Grand Bharat's courses were completed in 1996. A Golf Academy is attached to the resort, where you can book in for a lesson and swing analysis.

The golf club includes The Ridge, The Valley and The Canyon nine-hole courses. Following Nicklaus' design blueprint, Landbase India transformed barren land into lush fairways and greens with the help of organic nutrients from leaf mold, farmyard manure and Neem cake.

The Ridge and The Valley nines combine as a signature course of some note. The Indian Open was held here in 2000 and 2001.

The Ridge has fairways that narrow, favoring accurate hitting over distance. Three of its holes have water hazards running along one side of the fairway. The Valley is kinder to longer hitters, offering wider landing zones off the tees. The Canyon nine is one of the most picturesque in The New Delhi Capital Region, with views of the surrounding hills and mountains. A number of its par 4s are driveable but not without risk. Dave Finn summed up what is on offer: 'Each course offers a variety of short and long holes, with plenty of bunkers, strategically-located water hazards and undulating greens.'

OPPOSITE: View from the Valley Golf Course.

The challenges

On the championship course, undulating fairways that narrow towards the green, long water hazards, well-placed bunkers and some long par 3s.

The resort experience

ITC's philosophy is to create hotels that are 'rooted in the soil' and ones that show off the grandeur of India's heritage and culture. ITC Grand Bharat is in keeping with that – nationally-inspired architecture and interior design, and gracious Indian hospitality. The opulent hotel was voted Best Resort in Asia in *Conde Nast Traveler USA*'s Readers' Choice Awards in 2015 and 2016. The resort features 100 suites, four Presidential Villas and Kaya Kalp – The Royal Spa, a facility with nine treatment rooms that was awarded Best New Spa (Resort) at the GeoSpa AsiaSpa India Awards in 2016.

Type of grasses: Fairways have Tif 419 Bermuda grass and the greens Tif Dwarf Bermuda grass.

When to play: Open year-round, although it can get chilly in January. The courses are closed on Mondays.

Par: Ridge (36) – Valley (36) 72. Valley – Canyon (36) 72. Canyon – Ridge 72

Yardage: Ridge – Valley 7,114 yards, 6,505 metres Valley – Canyon 6,708 yards, 6,134 metres Canyon – Ridge 6,676 yards, 6,104 metres

Slope: Ridge – Valley 140, Valley – Canyon 134, Canyon – Ridge 134

Rating: Ridge – Valley 73.8, Valley – Canyon 71, Canyon – Ridge 71

Best hole: Hole 11 on the championship course (the Valley nine's hole 2) will challenge for distance, playing 224 yards (205 metres) off the back tees. The green sits on the left side of the slope with bunkers guarding it. There is out of bounds from tee to green and an element of risk and reward depending on pin placement. The hole consistently plays over par in championship events.

The pro says: 'The hillocks and knolls of the Aravallis lend themselves ideally to create enticing fairways, cunning greens and engaging waterways, which are enough to quicken any serious golfer's heart.'
– Priya Puri, Head Golf Professional, Classic Golf & Country Club

Dine and wine

Thank God for Indian food – you can have this and more at ITC Grand Bharat's five restaurants and two bars. Enjoy regional cuisine including Mewati Barbecues at Apas Promenade, European fare in The India Room and 'Swasthya' cuisine (eating for health and taste) in the Aravali Pavilion. The Peacock Bar is a good spot to unwind at the end of the night with a glass of fine wine. After your round, at the club house, the Nineteenth Hole specializes in serving fine spirits, or you can sit down in The Sandpit for lunch or dinner.

The accommodation

The Deluxe Suites (753 feet squared, 70 metres squared) offer a choice between terrace access or a lap-pool. I'm going with the lap-pool. The interiors are modern and classy. All suites are serviced by Retreat Hosts that aim to go beyond what a traditional butler service offers. Short of hitting the golf ball for you, that sounds good. The Presidential Villas (5,726 square feet, 532 square metres) come with a personal chef, which is fine provided he knows when it's bedtime. There's also a dip pool and jacuzzi, a sauna in the bathroom, and an elevator that takes you to two bedrooms on the first floor.

ABOVE: Apas Promenade and Pool.

OPPOSITE ABOVE: Apas Promenade; *BELOW:* Master bedroom.

Other activities

Kay Kalp spa features a 90-minute Golfer's Recovery treatment that sounds appropriate. Deep tissue massage with warm herbal poultices aim for your sore spots and loosen your muscles. The acupressure scalp and foot massage help rejuvenate the body.

For those keen on getting busy outdoors, take a Segway tour, go zorbing (rolling down a hill inside a giant ball), or try some badminton, squash or tennis at the resort.

Jakobsberg

Rhineland-Palatinate, Germany

Jakobsberg

Location: Im Tal der Loreley, 56154 Boppard, Germany
Website: www.jakobsberg.de/en
Phone number: 49 0 6742 8080

Sitting on a plateau above the famous Lorelei Valley in Germany's central west, Jakobsberg is your classic high-end golf destination. As the Rhine River winds its way through vineyards and forests a short distance below, you'll be teeing off on a course that has great views down into the Rhine Valley.

The 1st hole looks across to Marksburg, one of the most impressive castles in the Rhine Valley, according to German golf writer Ulrich Mayring. 'It is your aiming point for the second shot on the par 5 1st hole.'

But there is a great variety of holes on offer here – some with outstanding views, others more secluded – that will test all your shots. Dubbed 'Yellow Waterloo', the 210-yard (192-metre) hole 3 will see you hitting over a gorge for a narrow, undulating green. You'll face another gorge on hole 6, the 'Grand Canyon', where your tee shot must carry between 142 yards (130 metres) and 196 yards (180 metres) to the fairway, depending on how much of the dogleg you are trying to cut off. The 459-yard (420-metre) 'Mission Impossible' – or hole 15 – will challenge you for distance to make par 4.

'You'll have to shape the ball off some tees and bomb it off others,' said Mayring. 'You can score very low if your game is on. But they can make the greens very difficult, too.'

The course, which opened in 1994, was based on plans by American architect Robert Trent Jones Jr, but local designer Wolfgang Jarsombek built the course.

'Even though the course doesn't have any fairway irrigation, it is very playable year-round and has a super fun factor.'

The challenges
You'll have to navigate around large bunkers and five water hazards. The greens are fast and undulating, but if your game is on you can score low here.

The resort experience
The Jakobsberg was originally built by Emperor Frederick I in 1157 as a monastery, which is why you'll find a beautiful chapel on the estate. When Dr. Hans Riegel – a German entrepreneur who started the popular confectionery brand Haribo (think Gummy Bears) – developed the site into a modern four-star hotel, he preserved

OPPOSITE: Jakobsberg Golf Course.

the monuments and historic buildings. You'll find examples of Riegel's passions through the hotel – whether it be mounted hunting trophies, artworks by Benetton or ballooning. A shop also sells Haribo sweets so the kids will be happy.

'I've played there on almost 30 occasions and my non-golfing wife has never once been bored,' said Ulrich Mayring.

Dine and wine

Ask for a window seat at the Jakobsberg restaurant and you'll have a view of the Rhine's hairpin curve at Boppard. Or, if the weather is fine, head out to Rhine terrace and eat al fresco. It's not a bad spot to enjoy some game specialties fresh from the hunting grounds on the estate. And try a drop of the dry Dornfelder from the hotel's own vineyard, too.

You can pick between the Montgolfière and Gallery Safari bars if you just want to drink and chat, too. Flight's End, a glass pavilion at the club house, has a bistro and light snacks once you've completed your round. Sit back and enjoy the view.

Type of grasses: Tees are a mix of fescue grasses, fairways are Lolium perenne ryegrass and greens are a blend of bentgrass and poa annua.

When to play: The course is open most of the year but can be hit by snow and freezing conditions from December to February. Despite the exposed plateau location the wind is usually not too bad.

Yardage: 6,507 yards, 5,950 metres

Slope: 131

Rating: 71.1

Best hole: Hole 16, 'View of the Rhine', may be the easiest hole on the course but it comes with the best vista of the valley. Soak it up before you hit your tee shot 214 yards (196 metres) down the hill and onto the green from the back tee.

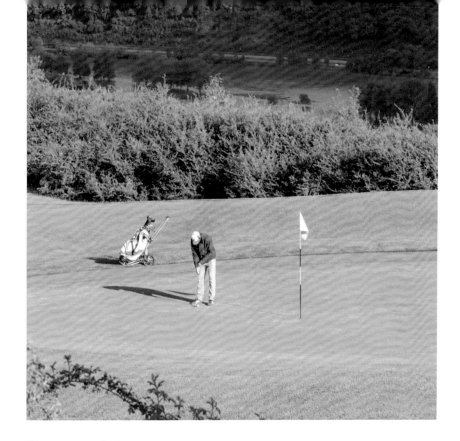

The accommodation
The comfortable rooms range from small single to a more spacious suite with living room and whirlpool. You'll find them decorated with one of three themes: Benetton, African safari or Montgolfière (ballooning). Most have a terrace or balcony to enjoy the view.

Other activities
The upper Middle Rhine Valley is listed as a UNESCO World Heritage site filled with historic towns, castles and vineyards to visit. History buffs will love exploring this region, which has been one of Europe's most important trade and transport routes. Try cycling down the Rhine cycle path or hiking to the nearby Ehrbach Gorge near Schöneck Castle.

A variety of hunting expeditions for roe buck and wild boar can be booked in nearby hunting ground in the Lorelei Valley. You can also test your accuracy with clay pigeons in the shooting range. Pull!

ABOVE: Jakobsberg Golf Course.
OPPOSITE ABOVE: Hotel Exterior; *MIDDLE:* Dining Room; *BELOW:* Indoor Pool.

Kauri Cliffs provides great coastal views as you play.

Kauri Cliffs

Northland, New Zealand

Kauri Cliffs

Location: 139 Tepene Tablelands Road, Matauri Bay 0478, Northland, New Zealand
Website: www.kauricliffs.com
Phone number: 64 9 407 0010

You know you've reached a certain level of opulence when the place you are staying at offers a helicopter transfer in its own private aircraft. Fly or drive to Kauri Cliffs from Auckland and you will be rewarded with one of the most scenic and interesting golf courses in New Zealand. The resort is owned by American billionaire Julian Robertson and is a sister property to his other luxury lodges: Cape Kidnappers in Hawke's Bay and Matakauri in Queenstown.

Kauri Cliffs is set on the high rolling hills and cliff tops overlooking the blue water of the Pacific Ocean at Matauri Bay in the north-east of New Zealand's North Island. The course was designed and built by the late American architect David Harman in 2000 and was more recently renovated by Rees Jones, who made the 5th hole a short drop-shot par 3 with a green flanked by five bunkers.

The front nine winds its way down lush rolling hills to cliff tops overlooking the ocean, hitting over gullies as you go. It's stunning coastal scenery. The first part of the back nine sees you descend into valley farmland, hitting over marshes and avoiding trees before the fairways climb the escarpment again. I was happy to belt a 3-wood onto the green 515-yard (471-metre) hole 17 called 'Rainbow'.

Kauri Cliffs was ranked 49th in *Golf Digest's World's 100 Greatest Courses 2016–17*, and has hosted the Kiwi Challenge, a PGA Tour Challenge event, in 2008 and 2009.

Most people fly into Kerikeri and get a transfer but it is possible to take a scenic and windy highway north from Auckland (a four-hour drive). Once you arrive, you will find a picturesque farmland setting and a course with some truly challenging holes, especially when the prevailing wind picks up from the south-west.

Control the ball off the tee and you can score well here. Most of the course follows a links-style and there is plenty of room to use your driver.

After taking on the Kauri Cliffs professional golfers Cameron Barnes and Sebastiano Galeppini, I was soundly beaten on both the back and front nine. But it didn't matter – it was such a beautiful spot to play and enjoy some challenging holes, hitting over canyons, lakes and great elevation changes. I took almost as many photos as putts.

The highest holes on the golf course on the back nine offer a great vantage point to see of Cape Brett and the Cavalli Islands. Kauri Cliffs is a working farm so you'll

OPPOSITE: Kauri Cliffs – Hole No. 7

enjoy farmland views on the 6,000-acre (2,428 hectare) property, which maintains some 2,000 ewes and 4,000 lambs as well as up to 1,000 head of cattle.

The challenges

The undulating greens are fast but consistent. I rolled back off the 18th green with the wind after a decent bunker shot. Some nasty tall fescue will be a challenge to hit out of if you err passed the first cut. Carrying the ball over canyons (such as the 219-yard / 200-metre carry on hole 18), gullies, marshes and bunkers is all part of the fun.

The resort experience

You can expect absolute luxury here. The Lodge, where dinner and breakfast are served, has a stunning outlook over the golf course to Matauri Bay. You can choose to eat outside and enjoy this 180-degree panorama or inside in the lounge, card or dining rooms. The Lodge is luxuriously decorated without being opulent. It looks like a generous country homestead on the outside – but this one has a pro shop downstairs.

Type of grasses: Bentgrass on greens and tees; ryegrass on the fairways.

When to play: Year-round.

Par: 72

Yardage: 7,139 yards, 6,528 metres

Slope: 144

Rating: 74.8

Best hole: From the championship tee on hole No. 7, 'Cavalli', you'll be hitting over a deep gulley that falls away into the Pacific Ocean on this par 3. It's 220 yards (201 metres) to the green with the wind often moving the ball back towards the sea. The green has two bunkers in front and one on the right side. Enjoy the view of Pink Beach and the Cavalli Islands from the tee.

The accommodation is separate and feels secluded as you move down a path surrounded by totara forest. Cottages are split into two guest suites with a total of 22 suites available, so it won't ever feel overcrowded here.

It is easy to see why readers of *Travel & Leisure Magazine* (USA) voted Kauri Cliffs the No 1. Lodge/Resort in Australia, New Zealand and the South Pacific.

Dine and wine
Gents require a jacket for dinner, but the staff will loan you one if needed. Drinks and appetizers are served in the sitting room.

The accommodation
There are six standard suites and 16 deluxe suites. They feature an open fireplace, generous-sized bedroom and en suite bathroom with a giant tub and twin vanities. I can recommend soaking in the tub after a solid round of golf. The balcony is a great place to relax and take in the view. The bed and pillows are amongst the most comfortable I've slept on. The deluxe suites only get larger and more splendid. There's also a two-bedroom Owner's Cottage available when Mr Robertson is not visiting.

ABOVE: Lodge at dusk.

OPPOSITE ABOVE: Suite Sitting Area; *LEFT:* Veranda Dining; *RIGHT:* Ensuite.

Other activities

There is an assortment of fun outdoor activities during the summer. On Monday, you can take a guided walk to see native birdlife on the farm. Tuesday, participate in a putting competition with the golf pros as you drink cocktails. Wednesday features a pre-dinner haka by Kerikeri's Kapa Haka. On Thursday, you can take a morning tour of the farm. Then Friday, the Lodge staff will transport you down to Pink Beach for a swim and dinner that will feature lamb, grilled seafood and local produce, including wine and cheese. Picnic hampers can be arranged for a private outing to one of the secluded beaches, too. Guests can also go fishing, mountain biking, surfing or play tennis.

The Spa's signature treatments include a Kiwi Mud Wrap with thermal mud cocoon, facial and scalp massage, or Manuka Honey Healing Cocoon, which uses local honey for the scrub. You'll forget about any double bogies in here.

Fuji Course – Hole No. 15.

Kawana Hotel

Shizuoka, Japan

Kawana Hotel

Location: 1459 Kawana, Ito City, Shizuoka 414-0044, Japan
Website: www.princehotels.com/kawana
Phone number: 81 0 557 45 1111

Sitting on the eastern coast of Izu Peninsula about two hours' train ride from Tokyo, Kawana Hotel has long been known for its golf. The resort has two courses set out along the shoreline of the Pacific Ocean – Oshima and Fuji – but it is the latter that has developed a reputation as one of the best in the world. Fuji was designed by British architect Charles Hugh Alison and opened in 1936. The natural beauty of the site struck Alison when he was on vacation there in 1930, and he convinced hotel owner Baron Kishichiro Okura he needed a top-class golf course, according to a brief history provided by *Planet Golf**.

It is the mountainous topography next to the ocean and stunning views that set this course apart – on a clear day you can see the snow-topped, 12,388-foot (3,776-metre) Mount Fuji in the distance. The dramatic elevation changes start off the 1st tee, with the fairway dropping quickly before rising again by the ocean-side green on the 415-yard (379-metre) par 4. Two cleverly positioned bunkers are ready to gobble balls off the tee and on approach respectively.

The designer managed to bring out the best in the seaside location, using the landscape's features to create some exceptional holes. These include No. 7 (a 393-yard / 359-metre par 4 with a tight tee shot between the trees, undulating fairway and four bunkers that flank a small green), No. 9 (a 367-yard / 335-metre par 4 with a split fairway that climbs) and the scenic No. 15 (a 480-yard / 439-metre par 5 that plays alongside the ocean cliffs and has a tough shot that flirts with the water), according to *Planet Golf*.

Fuji Golf Course is ranked No. 64 in *Golf Digest's World's 100 Greatest Golf Courses 2016–17* and hosts the LPGA Japan Tour's Fuji-Sankei Ladies Classic Tournament each April. Japanese golf writer Masa Nishijima rated this the best resort golf course in Asia.

Kawana's Oshima Course was designed by Japanese architect Otani Mitsuaki and opened in 1928. It features some stunning ocean views but does not match Fuji in terms of layout. Both Oshima and Fuji are available only for hotel guests, and golf carts feature a GPS guide to help players with distances.

The challenges
The elevation changes, narrow tee shots and smartly positioned bunkers will test low-handicappers here, while dense foliage will swallow up balls from errant shots.

Fuji Course – Hole No. 11.

The resort experience

Kawana Hotel has an impressive and historic main building overlooking Sagami Bay. From the observation deck on the fifth floor of the Shin-Honkan Building, you can see over the two outdoor pools and golf courses and across to the island of Oshima. There are cool places to relax here. Hang out in the library with your favorite book or journal, shoot some pool in the billiard room, or go to the Mah-jong Room to play a Japanese version of rummy that uses tiles.

The pools are filled with water from Amagi Mountain and are open during the summer season, but you'll have to pay to swim unless you're under three. The large lap pool could be worth it.

Type of grasses: Korai grass – fairways and greens.

When to play: The warmer months are fine (Kawana's July average is 70° Fahrenheit or 21° Celsius, according to HolidayWeather. com **) but it would be too cold in December, January and February.

Par: 72

Yardage: 6,701 yards, 2,127 metres

Rating: 72.7

Best hole: The Fuji Course's par 5 hole 15 is the signature hole here. You'll be hitting from an elevated tee with the ocean on the left side of the dogleg left. Big hitters will take their ball over the water and tree line. Watch out for the fairway bunkers and trees along the way to a shallow green.

The designer says: 'The scenery resembles that of the French Riviera, but at not a single spot between the Italian and Spanish frontiers can be found so superb a combination of sea, cliffs, trees and mountains.' – Charles Hugh Alison *

Dine and wine

Guests have five options to choose from here, but I'd be booking into Inakaya first. The restaurant operates out of a 300-year-old country house and specializes in Japanese food. Elsewhere, you'll find the Main Dining room (French cuisine), the Grill (more casual fare), Sun Parlor Lounge (for tea, coffee and homemade cake) and Main Bar (cocktails and more).

The accommodation

Kawana starts with the Ocean View Twin Room A, with 436 square feet (40.5 square metres) and a balcony to chill out on, and moves through to a Suite Room with 803 square feet (74.6 square metres) including lounge area. The rooms come with all the typical amenities you'd expect from a top-class hotel and some extras. The kettle and refrigerator will come in handy.

Other activities

Take a trip to Akasawa Spa and relax your muscles in the hot spring as you take in the ocean views. It's approximately 30 minutes away by car. You might also want to take the scenic views offered from the top of Omuro Mountain, which you can ascend easily using the lift. It's about 25 minutes' drive from the resort.

*Source: Planet Golf (planetgolf.com.au)

**Source: www.holiday-weather.com/kawana_us/averages/

ABOVE: Exterior view of hotel.

OPPOSITE ABOVE: Japanese restaurant Inakaya; *BELOW:* A resort tempura chef.

Cougar Point Course,
Kiawah Island.

Kiawah Island

Kiawah Island

Location: One Sanctuary Beach Drive, Kiawah Island, South Carolina, 29455, USA
Website: www.kiawahresort.com
Phone number: 1 800 576 1570

Kiawah Island is a golf resort I'm excited to visit. This huge development lies on a bridge-connected island just south of Charleston on South Carolina's golden coastline. It became famous in the world of golf after hosting several major tournaments. There are five championship golf courses to play, each with unique challenges, designed by five of the biggest names in golf architecture.

The Ocean Course is the most prestigious, having been the site of the 2012 PGA Championship, which saw Northern Irishman Rory McIlroy raise up the Wanamaker Trophy. It was here that Bernhard Langer missed a crucial six-foot putt resulting in Europe handing back the Ryder Cup to the US in 1991, and the golf course where Irishmen Pádraig Harrington and Paul McGinley claimed the World Cup of Golf in 1997. It will be the site of the 2021 PGA Championship as well.

Indiana native Peter Dye and his wife Alice designed the Ocean Course in 1991, and it is known for being one of the toughest golf courses in the United States due to constant winds that blow over the layout as well as the fast greens and multitude of bunkers. There are views of the Atlantic Ocean along every hole here. The Ocean Course ranked No. 44 in *Golf Digest*'s list of the *World's 100 Greatest Golf Courses – 2016–17*.

Jack Nicklaus' Turtle Point Course features three impressive oceanfront holes. The layout was renovated under the Golden Bear's recommendations in 2016, adjusting greens, re-grassing fairways and tees with salt-tolerant Paspalum and rebuilding sand traps. Garry Player's Cougar Point (redesigned in 1996 and set for renovation in 2017) has gorgeous views of the Kiawah River, a constant presence on the front nine. It provided locations for the famous golf movie *The Legend of Bagger Vance* starring Will Smith and Matt Damon. There is a mix of risk-and-reward par fives, par 4s that will test you for distance and accuracy off the tee, plus tricky par 3s.

Osprey Point was created by Tom Fazio, and his layout winds its way through saltwater marshes, lagoons and forests. You might see the odd alligator sunning itself on the banks of a water hazard here. With generous landing areas off the tee, most out-of-play areas on the left and few forced carries, this is a friendlier course for the high-handicapper. Across the river on Johns Island, you can play Oak Point, a course designed by Carolina native Clyde Johnston that was renovated in 2015 with Paspalum grass. Carts are available for afternoon tee times on all courses.

OPPOSITE: **Osprey Point.**

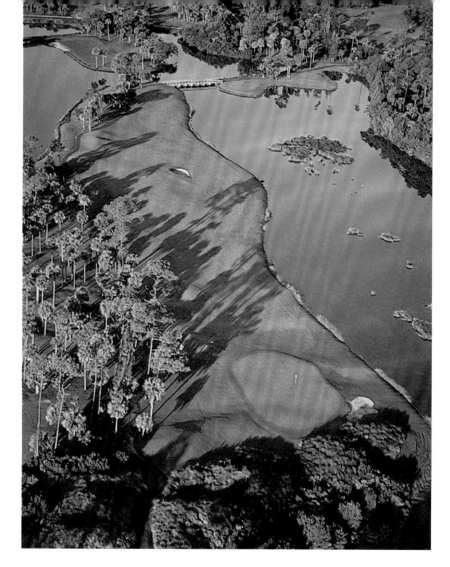

Type of grasses: Salt-tolerant Paspalum, which thrives on the oceanfront location, is on four of the five courses. Cougar Point closes after November 2017 for a 10-month renovation that includes conversion to Paspalum.

When to play: Year-round.

Par: All courses par 72

Slope / Rating / Yardage: The Ocean Course: 144 / 77.3 / 7,356 yards or 6,726 metres Turtle Point: 14 / 73.8 / 7,061 yards or 6,457 metres

Cougar Point: 137 / 73.3 / 6,875 yards or 6,286 metres Osprey Point: 135 / 72.8 / 6,902 yards or 6,311 metres Oak Point: 130 / 71.9 / 6,701 yards or 6,127 metres

The pro says: 'Don't go for the miracle shot. If you hit it in the dunes, take your medicine and get it back into play. Miracle shots are extremely rare on The Ocean Course and more often mean you'll be reaching into your bag for your next ball.' – Brian Gerard, Director of Golf, Kiawah Island Golf Resort

The challenges

The mountain to climb here is the Ocean Course. The windy conditions, bunkering, and slick greens and distance from the tips will mean you'll have to be in fine form to keep the score card respectable. The pro's tips: Employ a caddie and listen to the expert. 'Pete Dye is a master of making the player look the wrong way. On the tee box, many of the holes look like there's no place to land your drive but when you reach the fairway, you'll see it's 40–50 yards wide. Your caddie will know where to hit it.'

The resort experience

Kiawah Island is about 45 minutes' drive from the historic and beautiful Charleston, South Carolina. As well as being a special destination for golfers, Kiawah Island doubles as a tennis resort. It has two tennis centres, each with 12 courts, and has also been ranked the No. 1 tennis resort six times since 2016 by TennisResortsOnline.com. With plenty of calories burned between golf and tennis, it's a good thing that Kiawah Island has 18 dining outlets to choose from, of varying price-point and specialty.

When it comes to accommodation, you can retire to The Sanctuary, a 255-room, five-star/AAA Five Diamond oceanfront hotel. That, or choose one of the 450 luxury villas (one- to four-bedroom) or one of the 90 private homes to rent (three- to five-bedroom). With the warm South Carolina climate, I'm glad The Sanctuary has two outdoor pools and an indoor pool with Hydro Toning Fitness Classes. But you may just want to chill out on the highly-rated beach out front – just ask the concierge for a chair and umbrella.

Among many plaudits, Kiawah Island has been named: *No 2 – Best American Beach Resort* by *Conde Nast Traveler* in 2014 and *No. 4 – Top Golf Resort in the World*, by *Andrew Harper Travel Readers' Choice* in 2013.

Dine and wine

All the culinary options you could hope to find at one resort are here. I'm interested to see what a T-bone from a AAA Four Diamond/Forbes Four Star steakhouse tastes like. I'll find out in The Ocean Room at the Sanctuary. Otherwise I could choose Tomasso for Italian, the Cherrywood BBW and Ale House, Southern Kitchen for some authentic southern cooking, the Atlantic Room for Seafood, or the Ryder Cup Bar for some pub 'grub'. The list goes on.

The accommodation

It is five-star luxury from the Stand Guestroom (520 square feet, 48 square metres) up. Even this basic option, with its light, classic interiors and elegant furniture, has a king-size bed, a balcony with ocean views, and a five-fixture bathroom (including dual vanities, marble shower and deep bath tub). The Presidential Suite has 3,000 square feet (279 square metres) and includes a marble-tiled foyer, dining room and two balconies.

Other activities

The resort's coastal position means that there are plenty of activities to enjoy on the water at the beach or in the marshland that wraps around the island. You can surf, kayak, mountain bike, fish or paddleboard. You can also choose to go boating or take a nature excursion. It's hard to ignore the 24 tennis courts at the resort either. When you are exhausted, retire to the Kiawah Island Spa, which has been rated as one of the best in the United States by *Travel + Leisure* and *Conde Nast Traveler*. I think I'll get a Body Rescue and Citrus Head-To-Toe Massage.

OPPOSITE ABOVE: Ocean Course – Hole No. 6 green; *ABOVE:* Sanctuary Suite.

Bunkers surround the 8th green.

The Kinloch Club

Taupo, New Zealand

The Kinloch Club

Location: 261 Kinloch Road, Taupo 3377, New Zealand
Website: www.thekinlochclub.com
Phone number: 64 7 377 8482

Jack Nicklaus designed this course in 2007, but it wasn't until 2016 that a luxurious resort was completed to take full advantage of a remarkable location overlooking .Lake Taupo – New Zealand's largest freshwater lake in Central North Island. Although it looks like a classic Scottish or Irish links course in between green hilltops, Nicklaus has merged elements of links-style and parkland design to produce a beautiful and fun challenge for golfers. In typical fashion, The Golden Bear has used dozens of bunkers flanking the fairways and in front of greens. I counted twelve bunkers on the par-4 1st hole and managed to land in two of them for a double bogie. If your errant shot doesn't make it into a sand trap, then your ball could be in the long fescue.

'Opt for accuracy from the tee, not length,' said Kinloch Club Golf Director Tom Long. 'Don't attempt a 'superman' recovery shot following an errant shot – rather get the ball back in play and take your medicine.'

Significant elevation changes throughout the course mix up the approach shots, and provide some great views off tee blocks. The approach shot on hole 9 must climb a large hill with a bunker just in front of the green. Hole 10 then starts with a spectacular view over Lake Taupo. The par-5 16th offers a variety of approaches with a fairway split three ways and a valley that long hitters can carry over in two well-struck shots – a birdie opportunity that I welcomed. In general, however, you are punished for attacking the course. A sign in the clubhouse warns golfers just that: 'If you fight this golf course, it will beat you!'

The challenges

There are 172 bunkers along the fairways and greens. The greens are protected from the front so you'll have to take the aerial route on approach. As a rule, use one club up as there is more room at the back of the greens than the front. You'll be hitting over water on the par-3 3rd hole and around a lake on the 18th. The greens can be undulating and two-tiered but are not particularly threatening especially after those on 2,14 and 16 were redone during a renovation.

The resort experience

The Lodge at Kinloch is built on a hill overlooking the back-nine holes of the Nicklaus course and Lake Taupo. The main building is striking in its modern design, which has castle-like elements including a gangway entrance and central courtyard. But the

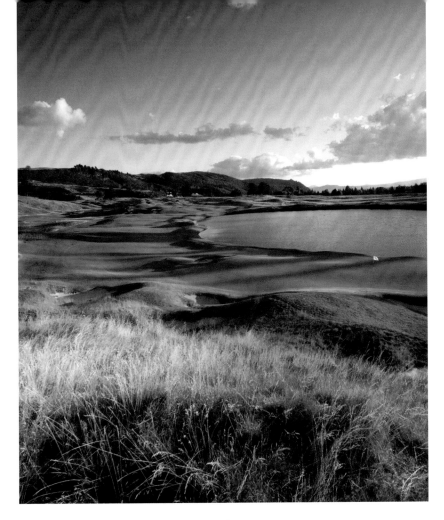

ABOVE: Kinloch Club – the approach to Hole No. 18's green.

Type of grasses: Tees are Princeville bentgrass, roughs and fairways are a mixture of fescue, while the greens are creeping bent and Bermuda grass.

When to play: Year-round, Tuesday to Sunday, although it can get rather chilly on winter mornings in July and August.

Par: 72

Yardage: 7,363 yards, 6,734 metres

Slope: 139

Rating: 77.4

Best hole: The 18th hole plays away from Lake Taupo and towards the impressive resort building. The fairway on the par 5 doglegs to the right before wrapping around a lake on the left-hand side. Players are invited to shoot over water on approach to make a birdie.

The designer says: 'It's a heck of a test. Aesthetically it fits right into the landscape, the bunkers have great shape.' – Jack Nicklaus * interior decoration offers some softness, with fox furs, goat furs, leather chairs and sofas. The Dining Room, the Great Room, Bar and Den make full use of the views while the Spa and Wellness Centre can be found one level below. There is a feeling you're in an exclusive place as your host offers pre-dinner drinks and you meet the other guests. Set in 628 acres (254 hectares) of peaceful land, you are also away from it all here.

Dine and wine

Some of the finest cuisine I've consumed in New Zealand was dinner (spinach and tomato soup, a delicious salmon plate and perfectly cooked beef main) and breakfast (delectable fruit plate before a hearty mix of sausages, scrambled eggs, hash browns and bacon) at the gourmet restaurant. I enjoyed the panoramic views of the lake and course as I tucked into these dishes, which have been prepared using produce from the 4,942-acre (2,000-hectare) home owners' estate. Each course is matched with fine New Zealand wine.

The accommodation

There are 10 two-bedroom villas, eight with duel keys so that they can be split into separate one-bedroom villas. Once you get past the giant doors, you'll find absolute luxury inside. Rest in front of the fireplace or take in the views of Lake Taupo on the terrace. Modern design and creature comforts are included such as the heated towel rails and bathroom tiles, and an enormous standalone bathtub. The comfortable king-size beds can be split into twins. One-bedroom villas have a full kitchen and courtyard for outside dining. Two-bedroom villas include two furnished terraces, laundry facilities and two bathrooms.

Other activities

New Zealand has some of the best fly-fishing in the world so I'll be wetting a dry fly the next time I'm in the Lake Taupo region. The resort provides trout fishing guides that take you to secluded spots by road or helicopter. They'll help with fly selection and spotting big browns and lovely rainbows. The Lodge's chef can cook up your prize trout once you return. All fishing equipment and a gourmet picnic lunch with drinks can be organized.

As well as the spa and tennis at the resort, you can go bungy-jumping into the nearby Waikato River, take a jet boat to Huka Falls, set out mountain biking, enjoy a scenic helicopter flight or skydive next to Lake Taupo. As Nicklaus said: 'You're in the middle of everything; the best fishing, hunting, water sports, skiing, the wilderness and mountains.'*

*Source: www.kinlochgolf.co.nz

OPPOSITE ABOVE: Kinloch Club Bar; MIDDLE: The Lodge view to Lake Taupo; BELOW: Bedroom Interior.

La Mer Course – Hole No. 2.

Le Touquet /
Le Manoir Hôtel

Le Touquet / Le Manoir Hôtel

Location: Avenue du golf, 62520 Le Touquet, France
Website: letouquet.com ; letouquetgolfresort.com/en/our-hotel/le-manoir-hotel/
Phone number: 33 03 21 06 28 28

Le Touquet Golf Club is one of the best golf destinations in Continental Europe. Located between a forest and dunes on the Opal Coast of north-west France, it features two championship courses that take advantage of the diverse environment. La Mer is a classic Scottish links-style course designed by British architect Harry Colt and built in 1931. It has hosted the French Open several times, the most recent of which the great Seve Ballesteros won in 1977. Elevated tees provide lovely views of the sea. La Forêt is laid out in the Le Touquet pine forest, which offers a more sheltered experience than the windy dunes. It was designed by fellow Englishman Horace Hutchinson and opened in 1904. The tranquility of the wooded course was broken when part of La Forêt was damaged in World War I. And again, as the Second World War intensified and Allied forces made landfall in France during June 1944, buildings surrounding the courses were bombed.

The courses have more recently undergone some major renovations to improve them for the modern game.

Independent website Top100golfcourses.com ranked La Mer as the 13th best course and La Forêt as the 54th in France in 2017. And 9-hole course Le Manoir – which was built in 1994 – is ideal for a quick hit in the late afternoon or a warm-up before the other courses.

The resort is about two hours' drive from Paris and you can check into Le Manoir, the historic on-site hotel that overlooks the golf courses.

'From a purely golfing point of view this is the best spot in Continental Europe that I've been to,' said German golf writer Ulrich Mayring. 'In the area, you'll have another world-class course in Hardelot Les Pins (designed by Tom Simpson) and if you venture an hour south there's the hidden gem Golf de la Belle Dune.'

The challenges

For La Mer you'll have to pay attention to the winds that whip off the English Channel and over the dunes. There are plenty of large bunkers to avoid, too, and fast greens. La Forêt has wider fairways but you'll have to land the ball on smaller greens.

OPPOSITE: The La Forêt course.

The resort experience

Le Manoir Hôtel was the family home of Allen Stoneham, the founder of Le Touquet Golf Club, and the charm of the original early 20th-century manor remains. It's a beautiful location: The hotel is surrounded by the Le Touquet Forest and overlooks the golf courses with the sea in the distance. The grand building was bombed during the Second World War in 1944. Following the conflict, it was transformed into a hotel to accommodate a growing number of golfers, according to manager Emmanuelle Christmann.

'Though the hotel suffered a lot during the War, Vincent Stoneham (son of Allen) and his wife Jean undertook a series of renovations and reconstructions to be able to satisfy a growing clientele,' he said. 'Le Manoir Hôtel is the perfect place to stay for golfers as its position opposite La Forêt course makes it very easy and handy to take the bag out and walk to hole 1.

Type of grasses: The fairways and greens on all courses are a mix of bentgrass, fescue and poa.

When to play: The courses are open year-round, although it gets close to freezing during January so you may want to play when it warms up.

Par: La Mer 72; La Forêt 71

Yardage: La Mer – 7,032 yards, 6,430 metres. La Forêt – 6,314 yards, 5,774 metres

Slope: La Mer 139. La Forêt 130

Best hole: Although La Mer's sequence of holes from the 9th to the 11th are memorable, hole 10 – a 152-yard (139-metre) par 3 – stands out. La Forêt's 497-yard (454-metre), par-5 hole 11 will test you.

'The place being heavily marked by history, the hotel architecture is a blessing to old times, the bar fully inspired from English pubs.'

Golfers can also enjoy the facilities of the relatively new club house, which opened in 2016, Emmanuelle said.

'The Spoon, as it's called, welcomes players (and non-players) to enjoy a fantastic view over La Forêt course. Its terrace is positioned to offer sunlight all day long.'

Le Manoir Hôtel was named Best Golf Resort in France in 2015 by *Today's Golfer*.

Dine and wine

Restaurant l'Ecusson boasts of a high-quality cellar on the premises to go with à la carte menus inspired by seasonal products. The clubhouse also features a restaurant and English-style bar when you've finished playing.

The accommodation

The three-storey building has 41 rooms and suites. 'Le Manoir is only a three-star hotel, but you'll sleep (and pay) for a four-star and you'll eat for a four-star superior,' according to golf writer Ulrich Mayring. 'It's a great place for a couple to stay, but there aren't the amenities you'd need for a family with kids.'

Other activities

Take a dip in the outdoor swimming pool, which is open July and August, or take some racquets out for a hit on the tennis courts.

ABOVE: Le Touquet Golf Club and Le Manoir Hotel.

OPPOSITE ABOVE: Le Manoir Hotel Exterior; MIDDLE: Club House Interior; BELOW: Club House Dining.

View across the water to Faldo Course's 18th green and the Lough Erne Resort.

Lough Erne Resort

Fermanagh, Northern Ireland

Lough Erne Resort

Location: Belleek Road, Enniskillen, Fermanagh, BT93 7ED, Northern Ireland
Website: www.lougherneresort.com
Phone number: 44 0 28 6632 3230

Northern Ireland features some outstanding golf courses and Lough Erne Resort happens to have two of them. Located on a peninsula between Castle Hume Lough and Lough Erne in the northwest of the country, you'll find the Faldo Course, which was designed by England's six-time major winner Nick Faldo in 2009 and was ranked No. 3 in Northern Ireland by Top100GolfCourses.com in 2017, and Castle Hume, a course that has hosted 10 Ulster PGA Championships.

Faldo's course is a must-play for visitors to Lough Erne Resort, which European golf writer and President of the European Golf and Travel Media Association Jo Maes rates as one of the 10 best in the world.

'The Scene of a recent G8 meeting, this five-star resort offers traditional Irish charm wrapped in a modern cloak,' he said. 'You feel as if there were lakes everywhere – there are – and the tower-styled lodge suites are dotted along the shores of Castle Hume Lough.'

Faldo's course sets out along Castle Hume Lough and works its way through pine forest before heading to the Lough Erne side. The course record was set by former world No. 1 Rory McIlroy, who was attached to the club as the touring professional – he shot a 68 on the par-72 layout. It's a true challenge for golfers of all levels, according to Maes.

'It will make you long for that pint of expertly poured Guinness after you've navigated your way past all the obstacles put in front of you. Elevated tees, deep bunkers, water hazards, sloped greens... this course has it all and it will test you.'

It's a stunning course with 18 unique holes and 14 of them with views of the water, said course professional Lynn McCool. 'As you play the course you get a real sense of nature and challenge,' she said. 'As you complete the par-3 15th hole and walk to the back tee of 16, you pass what is locally known as The Faldo Turn. There lies in front of you one of the most breathtaking finishes in golf.'

The challenges

Accuracy and distance management are crucial on the Faldo Course. Holes play next to two lakes and wetlands so there are many water hazards to contend with, especially playing approach shots over water. Many deep bunkers protect the quick

OPPOSITE: Lough Erne Resort – Hole No. 6.

greens, some of which are almost surrounded by water. Pro's tip: Go with the safe option – don't be tempted to drive the green on any par 4.

Castle Hume has over thirty bunkers, numerous water hazards and seven thousand trees across its layout.

The resort experience

Located in the town of Enniskillen in County Fermanagh, this five-star resort overlooks the Faldo Course and Fermanagh Lakelands. The accommodation consists of 120 rooms and suites in multiple buildings on the property that have a striking Irish-round tower design. Due to its scenic location and the fine service on offer, Lough Erne attracts honeymooners and wedding parties as well as keen golfers. Interestingly, the resort features a Thai Spa – said to be Northern Island's only one – that has sauna, steam room, jacuzzi and infinity pool, all of which are complimentary for guests. Lough Erne was named 2010 Golf Resort of the Year by the Irish Golf Tour Operators Association.

Type of grasses: A mix of bentgrass, fescue, ryegrass and smooth-stalked meadow from tee to green.

When to play: Year-round.

Par: The Faldo Course 72 Castle Hume 70.

Yardage: The Faldo Course 7,167 yards, 6,562 metres. Castle Hume 6,204 yards, 5,673 metres

Slope: The Faldo Course 129

Standard Scratch Score: Castle Hume 69

Best hole: The Faldo Course's 351-yard

(321-metre), par-4 hole 10 is the standout. The green has been built out on a man-made peninsula on Lough Erne with water almost surrounding it. Big hitters are invited to go for it, but many will find the water. Castle Hume's signature hole is a short par 3 called Ely Island.

The designer says: 'I've played golf on every continent in the world and I can honestly say I am overwhelmed by the location and beauty of Lough Erne Resort.' – Sir Nick Faldo *

Dine and wine

Executive Chef Noel McMeel aims to use the freshest local produce each day for the meals prepared at Lough Erne. You'll find fine dining at the Catalina Restaurant, which has photos on its walls of World War II seaplanes that were based at the Lough on its walls. I'm hoping to be there on Monday for the seven-course tasting menu. If that doesn't work, I might try the Lough Erne Pork Dish, which has pork belly, pork fillet, pork cheek, ham hock, and black pudding palmier, washed down with a drop of Le Domaine D'Albas, Chateau d'Albas, 2014. (I'd be nervous if I was a Lough Erne hog). After dinner, settle in by the open fire with a glass of Irish whisky in the Gordon Wilson Library. Other eateries include the Blaney Bar, which has a grazing menu, and the Loughside Bar and Grill (enjoy prime Irish meats and views of the Faldo Course).

The accommodation

There are six options for travellers, starting with the Traditional Rooms, which have a homey Irish country-estate style to the interiors along with king-size or twin beds. At the other end of the scale, you can select a three-bedroom lodge suite, which has a striking turreted design. Inside you'll find en suite bathrooms for each room, dining and living spaces, a claw-foot bath and luxurious Irish bed linen.

ABOVE: Faldo Course – Hole No. 10. *OPPOSITE ABOVE:* Resort Interior; *BELOW:* Lough Erne Resort.

Other activities

The Thai Spa is a highlight at Lough Erne. Bathe in the infinity pool before taking a treatment such as the Age-Defyer Facial, Personalised Body Wrap or Hot Stone Massage. Outside the resort, fish for salmon and brown trout in the surrounding loughs and rivers, explore the Upper Lough on canoe, or visit a remarkable subterranean world at the Marble Arch Caves Global Geopark.

*Source: www.lougherneresort.com/the-faldo.html

Machrihanish Dunes – Hole No. 2 at sunrise.

Machrihanish Dunes
/ Ugadale Hotel

Argyll, Scotland

Machrihanish Dunes / Ugadale Hotel

Location: Machrihanish, Argyll, Scotland, PA28 6PT
Website: www.machrihanishdunes.com
Phone number: 44 01586 810 000

When I first listened to Paul McCartney sing Beatles' classic *The Long and Winding Road*, I had no idea there was a world-class golf resort at the end of it. The road is the scenic A83 from Glasgow and it leads through Loch Lomond and the Trossachs National Park and all the way to Campbeltown on the Kintyre peninsula on Scotland's west coast. Near to this seaside town, you'll find Machrihanish Dunes resort, which opened in 2009.

Machrihanish Dunes golf course was designed by local Scotsman David McLay Kidd, who worked with the Scottish Natural Heritage to retain indigenous flora on an undulating piece of land that was formerly grazed by cattle and sheep. The tees and greens were the only parcels of land that were manipulated – the fairways and roughs were cut down to produce a links course that flows with the land, bumps and all. It is billed as 'the world's most natural golf course'*. While you may not always see the fairway, you'll have a good view of the Atlantic from most positions on the course.

The combination of great golf, warm resort service at Ugadale Hotel and Cottages, and fresh local fare makes this one of the most highly desirable golf destinations in the country. The course itself was ranked No. 23 in *Golf World's Top 100 Golf Courses in Scotland* in 2015 and No. 24 by Top100GolfCourses.co.uk's *Top 100 Courses in Scotland* in 2017.

Once there, you'll want to play neighbor course Machrihanish Golf Club, which was designed by legendary Scottish champion Old Tom Morris in 1879. *Golf Digest* ranked it 91 in its list of *The World's 100 Greatest Golf Courses – 2016–17*.

The challenges

Unsighted approach shots, rough that is mowed by a flock of sheep, and bunkers in unlikely places. This is links golf 'au naturel' but best to keep your clothes on and the ball low to deal with the wind coming over the dunes from the Atlantic Ocean. The greenkeeper's advice – pay attention to the signage: 'Maps are provided on the walk between every green and tee that give players a perfect opportunity to study the hazards that they will encounter next.'

OPPOSITE: Machrihanish Dunes – Hole No. 2.

The resort experience

A variety of fine accommodation is available in a resort that is spread out between the golf course and nearby Campbeltown. The Ugadale Hotel and Cottages are closer to the 1st tee, in a beautiful natural setting by the Atlantic Ocean. The hotel is an historic building that has been carefully restored. It features the Serenity Spa, where you can indulge in a massage and beauty treatments. The stone cottages add a level of privacy and increased space for larger golf groups. You can also choose to stay in town at the Royal Hotel, another restored building that offers harbor views from every room plus a shuttle service to get you to the course. Golf Tourism Scotland named Ugadale Hotel the 'Best Hotel (21–50 Rooms)' in 2015 and 2016.

Type of grasses: The links fairways use the natural machair grasses of the land – creeping red fescue, highland bent and other natural species. The greens are a mixture of chewing fescue, browntop bent, creeping red fescue and poa annua.

When to play: 'Because Machrihanish is warmed by the waters of the gulf stream, it is among the warmest places in the UK,' said Head Greenkeeper Simon Freeman. 'The course drains very well, and we therefore have no problem keeping it open for play all year round. The weather can occasionally be very wild in the depths of Winter (December-February), but conversely it can also be surprisingly good.'

Par: 72

Yardage: 7,082 yards, 6,476 metres

Slope: 132.

Standard Scratch Score: 71

Best hole: The par-3 hole 5 plays from an elevated tee to a green perched on a sea wall. There are beautiful views of the village of Machrihanish.

The greenkeeper says: 'Like all links courses that are laid out over rolling topography, Machrihanish Dunes has a lot of exasperating hidden surprises that can catch out the unwary player!' – Simon Freeman, Head Greenkeeper

Dine and wine

Golf Tourism Scotland gave the Village at Machrihanish Dunes the Best Catering award in 2015 so you can expect excellent cuisine here. Each hotel features its own restaurant and pub, each with a unique menu. The Royal Hotel in Campbeltown has the Black Sheep Pub and Harbourview Grille where you can enjoy fresh seafood or seared steaks. The Ugadale Hotel and Cottages features the Old Clubhouse Pub, where I can envision myself enjoying a pint of local beer and telling long tales about my round as the music plays. For those opting for a more refined setting, The Kintyre Club offers gourmet cuisine and fine wines to members of the golf club and Ugadale guests.

The accommodation

The Ugadale Hotel hosted captains of industry and their families in its day but there is a homely and cozy look to the rooms. You'll find Classic Rooms with an interior of brown and red colors, with walnut wood and antique brass furniture. There's a TV and writing desk, and you can have a king-size or double bed. The suites come with a living room, sitting area, bathtub and views of the Atlantic and the 1st tee at the Machrihanish Golf Club.

Other activities

Cambeltown is a famous whisky-producing town. After my sports massage and facial at the Serenity Spa, there is no doubt I'll be signing up for a whisky tasting tour. The Ugadale can arrange a visit to Spingbank (Scotland's oldest family-run distillery), Mitchell's Glengyle Distillery (home of Kilkerran single malt scotch) and Glen Scotia. There are also nature walks to the Kintyre beaches and Machrihanish Playpark for the kids.

*Source: machrihanishdunes.com

**Source: www.telegraph.co.uk/travel/destinations/europe/united-kingdom/northern-ireland/articles/Rory-McIlroys-favorite-golf-courses/

ABOVE: Practice Green. *OPPOSITE ABOVE:* Old Clubhouse Exterior; *MIDDLE:* Ugadale Hotel; *BELOW:* Old Clubhouse Bar, Ugadale Hotel.

Mission Hills, Haikou – the approach on Black Stone Hole
No.2 with lava rock on the right and numerous bunkers.

Mission Hills,
Haikou

Hainan, China

Mission Hills, Haikou

Location: No.1 Mission Hills Boulevard, Haikou, Hainan, China
Website: missionhillschina.com/en-US/Haikou/golf
Phone number: 86 898 6868 3888 and 86 755 2802 0888

When it comes to golf in Asia, Mission Hills is one resort that often comes up first in a conversation with golf writers and experts. The brand is quickly growing in reputation as a golfing destination of the highest order – or should we say, destinations. An important thing to note is that Mission Hills has three locations with two close enough to form one giant development. Mission Hills, Shenzhen in the Guangdong Province features seven 18-hole courses designed by some of the great architects and most famous names in the sport, including the World Cup Course by Jack Nicklaus (par 72, 7,294 yards / 6,670 metres) and the Ozaki course (par 72, 7,024 yards / 6,423 metres) by Japanese legend Masashi Ozaki. Swedish great Annika Sorenstam's first course Annika (par 72, 6,703 yards / 6,129 metres) is one of the features of the nearby Mission Hills, Dongguan, which has five championship courses. It also has a course by Greg Norman (par 72, 7,228 yards / 6,609 metres) that aims to bring the challenges of Melbourne's sand belt to the Chinese resort.

However, renowned Japanese golf writer and design consultant Masa Nishijima rated Mission Hills, Haikou as the top golf resort in China. The mega development sits on the island of Hainan off the southern coast of the mainland and has been built on a bed of lava rock. Here you'll find 10 courses to choose from, each offering challenges inspired by some of the world's most famous layouts.

Sitting at the top of the list is the par-73 Blackstone Course, which hosted the World Cup of Golf in 2011. The 7,808-yard (7,140-metre) layout winds its way through dense jungle, over rolling hills and between Lychee trees and ancient lava flows. Americans Brian Curley and Lee Schmidt, who designed and built all 10 Haikou courses, decided to eliminate the rough and opt for fairway cut throughout, but golfers will be challenged by the distance, huge bunkers, as well as forced carries over lava rock.

Masa Nishijima's favorite Haikou course is Lava Fields (par 72, 7,475 yards / 6,835 metres), which offers a similar layout to the Blackstone Course with challenging bunkering, but with fewer trees it is much more open. The lush fairways are laid out between the black lava rock. Both Blackstone and Lava Fields are walkable (paths even go over the lakes so you don't walk around them). Other courses at this resort include the Sandbelt Trails, The Vintage, Stepping Stone, Meadow Links, Stone Quarry, Double Pin, The Preserve and Shadow Dunes.

ABOVE: Blackstone Course – Hole No. 2 approach.

Type of grasses: Greens are Platinum Paspalum while tees, fairways and roughs are Salam Paspalum.

When to play: Year-round. However, given the tropical climate, there can be heavy rains in summer (June-August) and autumn (September-November) is typhoon season.

Par: Blackstone Course par 73 Lava Fields Course par 72

Yardage: Blackstone Course 7,139 metres, 7,808 yards Lava Fields Course 6,835 metres, 7,475 yards

Slope: Blackstone Course 135 Lava Fields Course 131

Rating: Blackstone Course 75.6 Lava Fields Course 72.9

Best hole: Blackstone Course: hole six (598 yards, 547 metres), a par 5 dubbed 'Devil's Hole', has trees on the right off the tee and multiple huge bunkers surrounding the green. Lava Fields Course: the 513-yard (469-metre) 9th will test even the longest hitters to make par in 4 shots.

The course designer says: 'The two courses are very similar in their design 'playbook': Width, transitional, irregular turf lines and bunker edges, centre-line hazards that draw your eye, not crazy greens, and very walkable as well. Both are more bombers' courses than most. 'My favorite course to play is Shadow Dunes – sporty, short, very wild, huge greens. We created a dunes course on the lava rock.' – Brian Curley

The challenges

Blackstone Course is difficult off the back tee and you'll have to avoid the sprawling bunkers and trees to score well here. Lava Fields Course features similar bunkering but is more open to the wind and you'll be hitting over more volcanic rock. Both courses favor big drivers of the ball, with wide open fairways and little rough.

The resort experience

Mission Hills, Haikou is a giant development – not only in terms of the number of golf courses on offer but the resort itself is an 18-storey hotel overlooking the lush fairways. There are 539 luxury suites and rooms in the complex, and each has a balcony to enjoy the view. There are indoor and outdoor swimming pools as well as the Lava Lagoon aquatic theme park, which features a man-made beach, Lazy River, pool, and beach volleyball and soccer. While you're out knocking a ball around, the children can enjoy crafts in the Kids' Club (try the Origami or Calligraphy Workshops) and games room. The resort itself has received awards for its environmentally-friendly design.

ABOVE: Blackstone Course – Hole No. 15.

Dine and wine

No need to go hungry here. There are 12 restaurants to choose from including the Silver Moon, which features Hainan and Canton specialties such as the braised sea cucumber or Wenchang poached chicken.

The accommodation

You'll find everything from the Deluxe Room with 538 square feet (50 square metres) of space and broadband internet so you can stay connected, through to the Spa Villa with independent dining room, kitchen and steam room as well as an outdoor Jacuzzi. Rooms feature chic, modern interiors and a large flat-screen TV you can watch from your bed.

Other activities

There is nothing like easing the muscles in a spa after a solid round of golf, especially if you have burned calories walking. What makes Mission Hills Haikou stand out is that there are 168 hot and cold mineral spring pools to choose from – some are filled with herbs to assist with specific conditions, such as rosemary to help respiratory ailments or oregano for muscle inflammation. It is the 'World's Largest Mineral Springs Resort', according to Guinness World Records, with the facilities spread out over 1,897,505 square feet (176,284 square metres). The Mission Hills spa has hair and nail treatments, hydrotherapy and, interestingly, a library and café.

Passeier-
Meran Golf
Course.

Passeier-Meran /
Hotel Andreus

South Tyrol, Italy

Passeier-Meran / Hotel Andreus

Location: Kellerlahne, 3A, 39015 San Leonardo In Passiria BZ, Italy
Website: andreus-resorts.it/en ; golfclubpasseier.com
Phone number: 39 0473 491330

Passeier-Meran is a championship course I'd love to play, purely for its setting in the Italian Alps. There are breathtaking views of the surrounding snow-capped mountains as you hit your ball around the south side of the Passiria Valley.

The course, which was designed by Willy Moroder of MPS Golf Design, features seven water-lily ponds on a layout that sits on 148 acres (60 hectares) of agricultural land. Hotel Andreus, the connected resort, runs a golf school that caters for everyone from the humble beginner to the keen amateur – a smart way to sharpen your skills before heading out. PGA instructors take individuals as well as groups of up to six.

Passeier-Meran is super fun to play and has a long season despite being in the Alps, according to golf writer Ulrich Mayring. 'Once I arrived on a Friday and everyone was out playing, then it completely snowed in on Saturday and Sunday (about three-feet deep) and it opened for play again on Wednesday and was completely dry on Thursday,' he said. 'That's due to the steep drop-offs on all sides – it's a mountain course after all.'

There is a cable car from the parking lot to the clubhouse so you know you are in the Alps! Interestingly, the Hotel Andreus takes guests on free weekly tours to other nearby golf courses, including Lana, Eppan and Dolomiti, so you can sample more than one course in south Tyrol.

The challenges

Control your ball on the shorter par-4 doglegs. There are plenty of wooded areas after the second cut, water hazards, and both green-side and fairway bunkers to avoid here.

The resort experience

This is a top-tier luxury resort and spa that includes many services for the price of a suite, such as the gourmet dinner and breakfast buffet. It says a lot that the German Football Team stayed at the Hotel Andreus prior to lifting the FIFA World Cup in Brazil in 2014. We're not sure how well the team members hit a golf ball but as Ulrich Mayring points out: 'They can go anywhere they like; money is no objective for the German Football Association.'

OPPOSITE: Passeier–Meran Golf Course.

'It's not only a five star, but one of the best I've seen, because there is none of the high-end aloofness and stiff atmosphere. It's super relaxed and the owning family makes their presence felt in a very down-to-earth way.'

Dine and wine

You'll enjoy a welcome drink on arrival and then face a six-course gourmet dinner at the Panorama Restaurant. Sommeliers will recommend suitable wines to go with it. The breakfast buffet is also included for the price of the accommodation. Complimentary pie and cake are served in the afternoon at the fireplace bar. Other

When to play: Passeier-Meran is a three-seasons public course, closing in the colder months of January and February, which is also when Hotel Andreus is shut. However, golf in December is not unheard of.

Par: 71

Yardage: 6,333 yards, 5,791 metres

Slope: 132

Rating: 71.9

Best hole: The 17th offers a proper challenge with a water hazard in front of the green and

233 yards (213 metres) to the centre of the green. Hole 10 is another tough assignment, with a ravine to hit over that is a daunting shot for average players (don't try this into the wind) as well as a bunker directly in front of the green that you must carry on your second shot. Ulrich Mayring likes the par 5 16th where 'Average hitters can reach the green in two. It's extremely risky (Out-of-Bounds if you get the line wrong), but you can feel like Bubba Watson on this par 5 and putt for an eagle!'

highlights include the juices and fruits, vegetarian dishes and a demonstration kitchen with various themed nights including a Mediterranean evening.

The accommodation
Hotel Andreus features 73 suites ranging in size from 323- to 1,884-square feet (30- to 175-square metres). They are furnished with local woods and stones that suit the Alpine setting as well as a fireplace you can cozy up to with blankets. Free Wi-Fi and satellite television come as standard. There's also a separate bathroom and bidet.

Other activities
Set out on an impressive 75,347 square feet (7,000 square metres), the resort spa and wellness centre is one of the focal points of this resort. The area includes a Mediterranean park to relax in while you decide what treatment to have. The snow and ice room might wake you up, but your worries will melt away in one of the saunas (ceramic, aroma steam, herbal, vital or Finnish). You'll find many types of massage available too (haki, lymphatic drainage, sports, full body, reflexology, etc) and mineral and mud wraps.

The indoor swimming pool is connected to a gate and lovely outdoor pool, which is heated year-round. You can also do laps in a 108-foot (33-metre) pool, which is heated to a slightly lower temperature. Yoga, Pilates, meditation, water gymnastics and Shamanic relaxation are also on offer.

The hotel will provide a rucksack if you decide to hike around south Tyrol – there are at least two guided hikes a week. There are also five tennis courts and a beach volleyball court. Or try horseback riding from the on-site stables.

ABOVE: Passeier–Meran Golf Course.
OPPOSITE ABOVE: Dining room Interior; *MIDDLE:* Resort pool; *BELOW:* Accommodation interior.

Pebble Beach's majestic 7th, photo by Tom O'Neal. Pebble Beach Golf Links and its images and individual hole designs are trademarks, service mark and trade dress of Pebble Beach Company. Used with permission.

Pebble Beach

California, United States

Pebble Beach

Location: 17-Mile Drive, Pebble Beach, California, United States, 93953
Website: www.pebblebeach.com
Phone number: 1800 877 0597

When it comes to golf resorts, few come with the history and aura of Pebble Beach. The famous links course is laid out on California's Monterey Peninsula with stunning views of the dramatic coastline and the Pacific Ocean swell rolling into the rocky shoreline below cliff-top fairways and undulating greens. The bunkering is spectacular on this course, from the stunning 106-yard (97-metre) hole seven that sees you hitting directly into the teeth of the wind, to a cliff-top green with five sand traps surrounding it, to hole 15 with six fairway bunkers and three green-side bunkers, to hole 16's island bunker in the middle of the fairway. You'll be hitting over the ocean on hole 6 and 8, and putting next to it on holes 4 to 10, 17 and 18. The 18th fairway wraps its way around the shoreline as it doglegs to the left, with a long bunker on the left side your last hope to stop a ball headed to the water.

The Pebble Beach Golf Links has been ranked the No.1 public course in the United States by *Golf Digest* from 2003 until 2016 and No.12 golf course in its list of *World's Greatest Golf Courses – 2016–2017*.

What makes the standard of the golf course even more remarkable is that two inexperienced American amateur golfers designed the layout before it opened in 1919. The story goes that local property developer Samuel F.B. Morse decided to build a top course to make the real estate more attractive. He brought in Douglas Grant and Jack Neville, two top amateur Californian golfers, to come up with the layout – it was their first. Neville told the *San Francisco Chronicle* in 1972:

'It was all there in plain sight. Very little clearing was necessary. The big thing, naturally, was to get as many holes as possible along the bay. It took a little imagination, but not much. Years before it was built, I could see this place as a golf links. Nature had intended it to be nothing else. All we did was cut away a few trees, install a few sprinklers, and sow a little seed.'*

Pebble Beach Golf Links has since become the stomping ground for celebrities and the game's top professionals. That's in large part due to crooner and film star Bing Crosby, who hosted the National Pro-Am Golf Championship in 1937 for charity with his celebrity friends. After the war, the first Bing Crosby Pro-Amateur Golf Championship was hosted at Pebble Beach. It eventually turned into the AT&T Pebble Beach National Pro-Am after Bing's death, an event that has seen the likes of Sam Snead, Jack Nicklaus, Tiger Woods, Phil Mickelson and Jordan Spieth

OPPOSITE: Winter waves on Pebble Beach's 18th.

raise the trophy, plus everyone from actor Bill Murray, quarterback Tom Brady and singer Justin Timberlake take part. It is the one PGA event that perhaps best shows the reach of golf as a popular sport.

Pebble Beach has also hosted four US Amateur Championships and five US Open Championships (1972, 1982, 1992, 2000 and 2010) and is set to host this major again in 2019.

There are five golf courses at the resort: Aside from the Pebble Beach Golf Links,

Type of grasses: Pebble Beach Golf Links has poa annua greens and rye grass on the fairways and tees. The same combination is used on the Links at Spanish Bay and Del Monte Golf Course, Monterey. Spyglass Hill Golf Course has poa annua greens and a mix of bent and fescue on the tees and fairways.

When to play: You can enjoy the courses year-round, but the best months in terms of weather are the warmer ones, May through to October.

Par / Slope / Rating / Yardage: Pebble Beach Golf Links 72 / 143 / 74.7 / 6,828 yards, 6,244 metres
Spyglass Hill Golf Course 72 / 144 / 75.5 / 6,960 yards, 6,364 metres

The Links at Spanish Bay 72 / 140 / 74 / 6,821 yards, 6,237 metres
Del Monte Golf Course 72 / 125 / 71.6 / 6,365 yards, 5,820 metres

Best hole: Pebble Beach's 543-yard 18th is a spectacular finish; the fairway wraps around the shoreline as it doglegs left. It has the ocean on the left, two fairway bunkers on the right and then four bunkers surrounding the green.

The golf writer says: 'If I think about all the courses on the Monterey Peninsula in totality, I consider Pebble Beach to have the most number of jaw-dropping shots and backdrops in the region.' – Fergal O'Leary you'll find the exceptional Spyglass Hill Golf Course (opened 1966; designer: Robert Trent Jones, Sr), The Links at Spanish Bay (opened 1987; designers: Tom Watson, Robert Trent Jones, Jr. and Frank Tatum), Del Monte Golf Course (the oldest course west of the Mississippi River, opened 1897, designer Charles Maud), and the nine-hole, par-27 Peter Hay Golf Course (opened 1957, designers Peter Hay, General Robert McClure and Jack Neville).

The first part of the Pro-Am is also played at Spyglass and nearby Monterey Peninsula Country Club Shore Course. Spyglass, which takes its name and the names of its holes from children's classic *Treasure Island*, is the other must-play golf course at Pebble Beach resort. It's also regarded as one of the toughest challenges in the game, with a course rating of 75.5 and slope of 144. The layout starts with five holes that work their way between dunes with beautiful views of the coastline and nasty bunkers directly in front of greens, then the course heads into the Del Monte Forest with holes that feature a combination of tricky bunkering, narrowing fairways, numerous green-side ponds and elevation changes. Holes 6 ('Israel Hands', a dogleg to the right with five bunkers), 8 ('Signall Hole', a 399-yard/365-metre

ABOVE: Pebble Beach – Hole No. 18. *OPPOSITE:* The Lodge.

par 4 that goes uphill) and 16 ('Black Dog', a 456-yard/417-metre par 4 that doglegs to the right but has a tree blocking your tee shot on that side) are particularly tough. Spyglass was ranked No. 11 in *Golf Digest*'s list of *America's 100 Greatest Public Courses in 2015–16*.

The challenges

Pebble Beach's bunkering on fairways and around the green will take its toll on the scorecard. High winds off the Pacific can make it a truly challenging course. Spyglass can be brutal. The first five holes have bunkers in front of the greens, then the next 13 have a combination of narrowing fairways, elevation changes and green-side ponds and bunkers.

The resort experience

Pebble Beach has three separate resort hotels, including The Lodge at Pebble Beach, the nearby Casa Palmero and The Inn at Spanish Bay, which is about 10 minutes' drive from Pebble Beach.

The Lodge at Pebble Beach has been operating since 1919. This is a luxury hotel with a grand main building that overlooks the famous golf course and Pacific Ocean

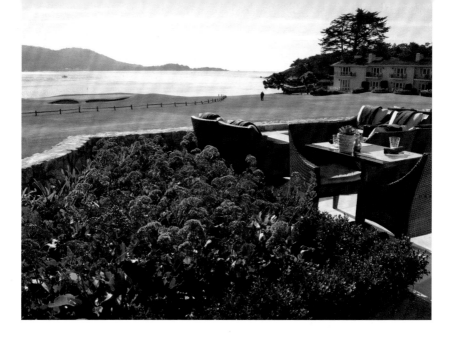

at Carmel Bay. Expect five-star service, accommodation, and facilities here. There are 161 stylish guest rooms, spread out across five buildings, on offer. The hotel features a spa, which uses herbs, plants and minerals from the Monterey Peninsula in its body treatments and massages. You can even receive a pre-game warm-up before you hit the links. The spa received the Forbes Five-Star Award between 2014 and 2016.

There are five restaurants at the lodge, too. Guests at the Lodge have access to the members-only Beach & Tennis Club and The Spanish Bay Club. The Lodge is dog friendly, too, and there is a dog day care for when you are out on the course.

Casa Palmero is a Mediterranean-style estate with 24 rooms, which each have fireplaces, king-size beds and giant tubs. The hotel has a library, billiard room and heated outdoor pool as well as a bar and lounge. The Inn at Spanish Bay has rooms with patios or balconies overlooking the pine forest, Pacific Ocean or fairways of the links course there.

Pebble Beach is approximately two hours' drive south from San Francisco International Airport and less than 20 minutes' drive from Monterey Regional Airport.

Dine and wine
The Lodge has five restaurants to choose from. Enjoy fresh seafood at the Stillwater Bar & Grill, a steak and beer at the Tap Room, a mix of meals prepared using open-flamed cooking and fine wine at The Bench, fresh coffee at the Gallery Café and a

BOTH: The Bench restaurant, The Lodge, all by Joann Dost.

cocktail by the fireplace at the Terrace Lounge (which also has great views of the 18th hole).

A short drive to the Inn at Spanish Bay, and you'll find six restaurants. Try the Pèppoli at Pebble Beach's Tuscan-style Italian, Traps for a cocktail or Toscana burger, or the Stave Wine Cellar for some fine wine in an intimate setting.

The accommodation

The Lodge at Pebble Beach has rooms that offer views of the Pebble Beach fairways, the garden, or Pacific Ocean. A Garden View (550 square feet, 51 square metres) features a marble bathroom, wood-burning fireplace and patio or balcony. You can opt for two queen-size beds or a single and king-size bed but all come with top-quality Egyptian cotton sheets. If you want to upgrade, try the single-bedroom Deluxe Ocean View Suite. It has a parlor with seating, a marble bathroom with whirlpool tub, an entertainment system and ocean views.

Other activities

As well as having a hot-stone massage and other such treatments in the spa, you'll want to check out The Beach and Tennis Club, which has tennis courts, a fitness centre and 82-foot (25-metre) heated pool and whirlpool spa. The Spanish Bay offers similar facilities for those staying on that side of the Monterey Peninsula. And for a bit of sightseeing, cruise down 17-Mile Drive and take in the dramatic coastline between Cyprus Point and Pebble Beach.

*Source: www.pebblebeach.com/golf/pebble-beach-golf-links/course-history/course-architects

The brilliant Pinehurst No. 2 – Hole No. 14.

Pinehurst

North Carolina, United States

Pinehurst

Location: 80 Carolina Vista Drive, Pinehurst, North Carolina, 28374, United States
Website: www.pinehurst.com
Phone number: 1 855 235 8507

Pinehurst is known as 'the Cradle of American golf,' which might seem a lofty tag until you get to know the history of this golf resort. Golf was in its infancy in the United States when entrepreneur and inventor James Walker Tufts had the idea to create a resort and village with multiple courses after purchasing 600 acres (243 hectares) of land in the sand hills of south-central North Carolina in 1895. The village became known as Pinehurst and the first course was completed in 1898. Tufts commissioned Scottish professional golfer Donald Ross to redesign No. 1 and add three new courses in 1900. Although Ross was not a proven architect, the meticulous Scot set to work creating courses that used the natural sandy ground to its full potential, weaving fairways between tall pines, building natural-looking bunkers and creating crowned greens with challenging breaks and slopes. Ross was a minimalist, using the features of the natural terrain and doing as little earth moving as possible to shape his courses.

There are now nine golf courses at Pinehurst, aptly named No. 1 through to No. 9. However, Ross's greatest achievement was Pinehurst No. 2, which opened in 1907 and still rates as one of the best courses in the United States. *Golf Digest* ranked it 63 in its list of the *World's 100 Greatest Course – 2016–17* and 30 in its list of *America's 100 Greatest Courses – 2017–18*. It best displays Ross's philosophy of giving golfers strategic choices.

The greens are fast, undulating and firm, with the highest point being in their centre and the slope falling away to the edges. Depending on the pin position, it can be difficult to either attack the flag or recover from a missed approach shot. The native sand, wiregrass and pine needles sit between fairways as the natural rough. Hole 16 is the only one where water comes into play. Renovation work was done on the course by R.T. Jones in 1974 and then by Bill Coore and Ben Crenshaw in 2010 to restore it to Ross's original natural character, eliminating rough that was introduced earlier, increasing the length to 7,565 yards (6,917 metres) and adding bentgrass to the greens.

Crenshaw loved Ross's design philosophy. 'He always thought Pinehurst No. 2 was for the expert player but still playable for the resort guest.'*

'Pinehurst absolutely was the pioneer in American golf,' Ross once said. 'While golf had been played in a few places before Pinehurst was established, it was right here in these sand hills that the first great national movement in golf was started.'*

Pinehurst has hosted more golf championships than any other site in the United

OPPOSITE: Pinehurst No. 2 – Hole No. 9.

Type of grasses: Greens are A1/A4 Bentgrass (mowed to 0.125in) and the tees and fairways are Tifway 417 Bermuda Grass (mowed to 0.4in).

When to play: Although Pinehurst is open year-round, the average temperature is chilly between December and February.

Par: 72

Yardage: US Open: 7,588 yards, 6,938 metres Blue: 6,961 yards, 6,365 metres

Slope: 138

Rating: 76.5

Best hole: A balanced course throughout, but the par-5 hole 5 is a beauty. Playing 576 yards (526 metres) from the back tee, the fairway turns to the left just before a green that has four bunkers on the edge of the fairway in front of it. The par-5 hole 16 (528 yards / 483 metres) is another tough battle – you hit over a water hazard as the fairway doglegs left. There are multiple bunkers to avoid. And hole 11, a 483-yard (441-metre) par 4, has been a critical birdie opportunity taken by tournament champions Payne Stewart, Michael Campbell, Michelle Wie and Ben Hogan, the latter having shot 3 four days in a row on his way to win the 1940 North & South Open.

States, with No. 2 being the battleground for the US Open in 1999, 2005 and 2014, the PGA Championship in 1936, Ryder Cup Matches in 1951, the US Women's Open Championship in 2014 (Michelle Wie won just after German Martin Kaymer took the US Open) and the US Men's Amateur Championship in 1962 and 2008. It has seen many of the greatest golfers over that 120-year period compete there, from Walter Hagen and Bobby Jones through to Tiger Woods and Rory McIlroy. It was the site of Ben Hogan's first championship win in 1940, after he edged out Sam Snead in the North & South Open, as well as being the stage for the famous duel between Phil Mickelson and Payne Stewart, which saw the latter make two incredible putts coming home to claim the 1999 US Open title. Robert Dedman, Jr, the CEO and owner of Pinehurst Resort, put it in perspective during a short documentary about No. 2.

'You get nervous when you are on that 1st tee, because you realize every great golfer of the last 100 years has played this championship course.'* Right, no pressure.

The US Open will return to Pinehurst No. 2 in 2024.

The challenges

On Pinehurst No. 2 you'll need to keep it on the fairway or you'll most probably be hitting out of sandy rough or wiregrass, both of which can provide tough lies. There are 111 natural-looking bunkers to avoid, especially around the crowned greens, which are fast, undulating and tricky. No. 2 is long from the back tees, too. Pro's tip: Take a caddie to help navigate Donald Ross's greens. 'These greens have been confounding the world's greatest players from all of the great eras of golf, and having some assistance in reading Ross's intricate and subtle manoeuvres will help considerably in the player's score.'

ABOVE: A room at the Carolina; *OPPOSITE:* The Carolina dining room.

The resort experience

Pinehurst resort is spread out across the small North Carolina village. The earliest marketing plan for the resort was as a health retreat that was enhanced by the Pine-scented air. That quickly changed when golf became more popular at the turn of the 20th Century, and the resort grew. There are now four hotels on offer: The Holly Inn, a Four-Diamond hotel that was built in 1895 and Pinehurst's original lodge that has afternoon tea at 4pm; The Carolina, a grand luxury hotel with 230 rooms nicknamed 'the Queen of the South'; The Manor Inn with the feel of a sportsman's lounge; and The Condos at Pinehurst, with two- or three-bedroom apartments that include a kitchen, private bathroom and living area for families or groups. The hotel buildings of The Holly Inn and The Carolina retain a classic southern style in their design.

The Spa at Pinehurst, housed in a beautiful white building, continues this classic look. There are 28 treatment rooms, steam room, sauna, and whirlpool spread across 31,000 square feet (2,880 square metres) here. Head to the spa for a four-hour treatment (with massage, pedicure, facial, manicure and lunch), or something from the 'Gentlemen's Menu' such as the sports massage. You can also opt to pay for a pass to use the lap pool and whirlpools. The fitness centre is complimentary.

The pro says: 'I've always thought that No. 2, from a design standpoint, has always been my favorite course in the country. Pinehurst is a totally tree-lined golf course, without a tree being strategically in play. Pinehurst just has so much in it, so much variety, it has so much character, it is just so much fun to play.'*
– Jack Nicklaus

'Donald Ross believed in providing golfers with strategic choices, and Pinehurst No. 2 was intended to epitomize that philosophy. In March 2011, No. 2 reopened following a year-long restoration project designed to restore the course's natural and historic character, and the strategic options that were the centrepiece of Ross's vision.' – Ben Bridgers, Director of Golf, Pinehurst Resort & Country Club

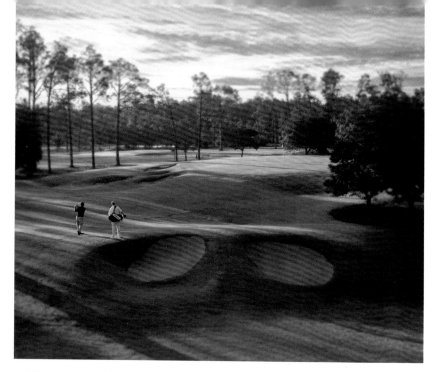

The accommodations, restaurants, golf courses, and activities are within easy walking distance or you can take the complimentary resort shuttle service.

Pinehurst is approximately two hours' drive east from Charlotte, or one and a quarter hour's drive southwest from Raleigh. Pinehurst received the *Golf Digest's Editor's Choice Award* in its list of *Best Golf Resorts in the Americas* in 2016 and *Golf Magazine's Platinum Medal Resort – 2014–15*.

Dine and wine

Being a resort village you can expect some variety here, and the nine restaurants should keep you satisfied. At the Carolina, the Dining Room has a buffet breakfast, and steak for lunch or dinner; The Ryder Cup Lounge features memorabilia from the 1951 matches played there, a fireside lounge and eight beers on tap (it's one of *Gold Digest's 50 Best 19th Holes*); and the Carolina Coffee shop is good for a sandwich or fresh brew.

The Holly Inn features the AAA-Four-Diamond 1895 Grille with seafood and Carolina-inspired cuisine, and The Tavern, which has an antique Scottish bar and a hearty pub menu. You'll also find the Donald Ross Grill, a favorite lunch spot for golfers, at the Resort Clubhouse. The 91st Hole here also has burgers.

Elsewhere, Course No. 7 has the Fairwoods Dining Room for Cobb salad, and Course No. 8 has Centennial Dining Room with a deli-style menu.

ABOVE: Pinehurst Hole No. 4; *OPPOSITE:* The 8th on Pinehurst No. 8.

The accommodation

All up there are 480 guest rooms across the three hotels as well as condominiums and villas.

The Carolina, which opened in 1901, is an elegant luxury hotel with grand architecture that sits on the National Register of Historic Places. The rocking chairs on the veranda look like a great place to relax with a whisky in hand. The Carolina has 230 guest rooms including a 1,600-square-foot (148-square-metre) Presidential Suite.

The Holly Inn is another place I'd love to stay. Although the wooden lodging was built in 1895, the 82 guest rooms have all the modern perks whilst retaining the elegant interiors and details. A Traditional Room has a king-size bed with feather top, Wi-Fi and TV.

You'll find more casual lodging at The Manor, which opened in 1923, with its 42 guest rooms. Those in large groups can opt for one of Pinehurst's four- three- or two-bedroom villas, each with a full kitchen.

Other activities

Apart from the nine golf courses to play here, if you have the energy you might try the highly-regarded tennis facility. It has 24 courts (six hard surface and 18 soft Har-Tru). Pinehurst also has two croquet courts, which have hosted the US Croquet Championship. The West Lawn Activity Centre has a hot tub, two pools, an outdoor fireplace and putting green.

Even better, head to Lake Pinehurst and Beach Club for action on the 200-acre (81-hectare) lake. Enjoy kayaking, fishing, swimming, sailing and canoeing. There's also a picnic area, beach volleyball, barbeque grills, and lifeguards watching over swimmers.

*Source: Pinehurst.com

Regnum Carya
Golf & Spa Resort

Belek, Antalya, Türkiye

Regnum Carya Golf & Spa Resort

Location: Kadriye Bölgesi, Üçkum Tepesi Mevkii, Belek-Antalya, Türkiye
Website: regnumhotels.com/en ; caryagolf.com ; nationalturkey.com
Phone number: 90 242 710 34 34

Regnum Carya is an all-inclusive luxury resort on Türkiye's Turquoise Coast, otherwise known as the Turkish Riviera. It has warm Mediterranean water lapping long beaches on one side and the Taurus Mountain Range adding a stunning backdrop on the other.

The history of the region is as fascinating as it is ancient, as nearby archaeological sites will attest to – Lydians, Persians, Macedonians, Romans, Byzantines, Greeks, Italians and finally Turks have been a part of it. It's fair to say none of those empires would have expected a world-class golfing destination would one day pop up in the sunny spot by the sea.

Approximately 25 minutes' drive from Antalya International Airport to the town of Belek, Regnum Cayra features two courses: The Carya Golf Club and the National Golf Club. Carya was designed by five-time Open Champion Peter Thomson in association with the Australian's company, Thomson, Perrett & Lobb Golf Course Architects. What sets this course apart from most is that it is floodlit for night golf – it's Europe's first floodlit course. The warm climate means that it's an entirely comfortable experience for resort visitors to play late into the night – the course closes at 12.30am.

Carya's layout tries to emulate old English heathland courses in the Surrey region, including The Berkshire, Wentworth and Walton Heath. It is a cross between links and parkland golf. The fairways are built on undulating sand dunes, but you'd never guess this with the lush greenery. Nearly one million heather plants were introduced to augment the heathland environment that was already there. Since opening in 2008, Carya Golf Club has hosted some major international tournaments, including the Turkish Open in 2016. In a healthy twist, players are invited to pick oranges from the trees in season. Top100GolfCourses.com ranked it as Türkiye's third best course in 2017.

The golf academy attached to the driving range features two teaching studios to help analyze and fix your swing, and a massive 164-yard (150-metre) putting green.

The National Golf Club was designed by Northern Irishmen David Jones and David Feherty and opened in 1994. The club was expanded to a 27-hole layout in 2015 and divided into the Irmark (1-9), Tuna (10-18) and Ada (19-27) courses. The

OPPOSITE: Carya Course – Hole No. 8.

fairways are laid out between eucalyptus and pine trees over rolling hills with the Taurus Mountains in the background. There are 64 bunkers and 10 lakes in play and forced carries on holes 2, 8, 21 and 24. Golfers must bring a handicap certificate to play the championship course. The National Golf Club hosted the Turkish Seniors Open in 1996 and 1997 on the European Tour. It was ranked Türkiye's seventh best course in 2017 by Top100GolfCourses.com.

The challenges

Carya offers golfers a free drop if you lose a ball in the purple-flowered heather so you are encouraged to rip your driver to the middle of the fairway and play a mid-iron second shot off the undulating fairways. The par 5s are hard to reach in two, and are well protected by bunkers and lakes. Take care on the slick and tricky sloping greens. The National has 10 lakes to navigate over or around.

Type of grasses: Carya's greens are TifEagle Bermuda grass and the fairways are Bermuda 419. The National has hybrid Bermuda grass on the fairways and a blend of Tifdwarf Bermuda grass and Poa trivialis on the greens.

When to play: Year-round. Bring something warm to wear in January and February.

Par: Carya – 72. National (Irmark-Tuna: 1-18) – 73

Slope / Rating / Yardage: Carya: 145 / 74.9 / 7,223 yards, 6,605 metres National: 134 / 72 / 7,031 yards, 6,429 metres*

Best hole: Carya 496-metre hole 10 – dubbed 'The Plank' – has a lake all the way down the left side and forest on the right side of the fairway. The approach shot will need to carry over a cove in the lake. The picturesque par-3 hole 8 and rooftop tee on hole 16 are standouts, too. The National's 127-yard (116-metre) hole 2 has a green almost surrounded by water.

The manager says: 'Inspired by some of the world's classic heathland courses, Carya Golf Club has designed a course that places a high emphasis on the strategic value of each and every shot.' – Hasan Ceylan, General Manager, Carya Golf Club

The resort experience

This all-inclusive resort packs a lot in for guests. It's a huge development that hosted a G-20 World Summit in 2015, but is just as likely to be a destination for those wanting a family vacation, sports-packed stay, or romantic getaway by the Mediterranean. You'll stay in five-star luxury rooms, have the choice of seven restaurants to dine at, get pampered at the Greendoor Spa (which uses organic products), get wet in an impressive aqua park with wave pool, family pool and a quieter adult pool, and relax under a cabana with a cocktail from the bar on the private pier.

Regnum Carya's theme is to get wet. There's an indoor pool and a giant heated outdoor pool by the hotel that will keep you swimming throughout winter, or you can relax at the resort's beach in the warmer months.

And that's for starters. I can't think of another golf resort that also has three FIFA-standard football fields (teams hold camps here). There are plenty of activities and sports (see below). Children of all ages are catered for in four clubs with impressive indoor (mini-disco, computer room, arts and crafts, maze) and outdoor play areas (forts, slides and sailing ship) plus a restaurant for kids and a non-alcoholic youth bar.

The resort's environmental credentials include LEED Golf Certification. Resort guests get a free transfer from the airport with direct bookings.

Dine and wine

Dining at any of the seven restaurants is included in the package for resort guests. The Gourmet Main Restaurant has buffet breakfast, lunch and dinner; Ristorante Tramanto serves Italian in a Mediterranean setting; Chufang entertains with Teppanyaki masters dishing out Japanese; The Seahorse has fresh fish by the sea; The Ottoman delivers traditional Turkish fare; Grill Do Brasil is a Brazilian steakhouse; and Sandal Restaurant serves Mediterranean seafood in summer.

ABOVE: Carya Course – Hole No. 15; *OPPOSITE:* Carya Course – Hole No. 11.

The accommodation

The main hotel building has 553 luxury rooms, with plush interiors and modern décor, overlooking the Mediterranean. The standard rooms of 667 square feet (62 square metres) – with French or twin beds, LED TV, separate bathtub, work desk, dressing room and balcony – can house up to three adults and one child. If you need a lot more room, the Presidential Sea View Suite (1,615 square feet, 150 square metres) has two bedrooms, two bathrooms, maxi bar, jacuzzi, coffee maker, a living room plus two large balconies. You can add privacy, a pool and go bigger in a Golf Room or Villa; the 37,637-square-foot (3,500-square-metre) Crown Villa has five bedrooms, a huge heated outdoor pool and a jacuzzi.

Other activities

Regnum Carya offers a huge range of outdoor activities and attractions. First, all guests have unlimited passes to the nearby The Land of Legends theme park, which has a water park with 77 slides, surf pool, crazy river, Typhooncoaster and 5D cinema amongst its rides.

Closer to the hotel, outdoor enthusiasts should try the Adventure Park (closed in winter). Located in a pine forest, it has zip lines, climbing walls, and an adventure track.

Of course, apart from the six pools on offer for all hotel guests and private pools, Regnum Carya also has Aquaworld (open May 1 to October 15). It features a 26,910-square-foot (2,500-square-metre) wave pool, a water games park, multiple pools, slides and a crazy river ride.

There are plenty of sports to participate in – from basketball and boccia to soccer and tennis – fitness classes such as Zumba and Pilates, as well as more artistic endeavors such as belly dancing and Latin dance classes.

*Source: www.golftop18.com/national-golf-club-review-turkey.html

Ritz-Carlton, Abama

Ritz-Carlton, Abama

Location: Carretera General, TF-47, km 9, Guia de Isora Tenerife, 38687, Spain
Website: ritzcarlton.com/en/hotels/spain/abama
Phone number: 34 922 126 000

Located on the Guia de Isora coastline of Tenerife in the Canary Islands, which sit in the Atlantic Ocean off Morocco, Ritz-Carlton, Abama could just be the perfect out-of-the-way luxury getaway for golfers. Tenerife is a volcanic island with the sometimes snow-capped Mount Teide at its centre, although the tropical climate also enjoys the most sunshine of any part of Spain – it is known as the Island of Eternal Spring, which sounds perfect for golf. It is also the most populated of the Canary Islands, with two international airports acting as thoroughfares for the tourist destination (the closest to the Ritz Carlton being Tenerife South Airport, approximately 30 minutes' drive away). But none of this will enter your mind as you tee off on the Abama Golf Course. This par-72 championship course was designed by the late Dave Thomas and opened in 2005. The Welshman was trying to create a European course similar to Augusta National in Georgia, according to course professional Brendan Breen. There may not be talk of moving the Masters to the Canary Islands any time soon, but Abama is a tropical treat for golfers just the same.

'The immaculately maintained 18-hole championship course contains over 300 species of subtropical plant life, including over 20,000 palm trees,' Breen said. 'Almost all the holes of the course have spectacular views of the Atlantic Ocean and the island of La Gomera.

BELOW: Citadel Koi Carp Pond; *OPPOSITE:* Abama Golf Course.

'There are 22 lakes spread throughout the course's ever-changing terrain, as well as waterfalls and white-sand bunkers.'

As well as the lakes and thousands of palm trees, perhaps the other feature to note is the elevation change across the layout. The course rises to 1,033 feet (315 metres) above sea level, making the GPS buggies essential for getting around, according to Carsten Fritz on Top100GolfResorts.com, which ranked this as Spain's 26th best course in 2017.

The course hosted both the Abama Open de Canaries European Tour event in 2005 and Tenerife Ladies Open on the Ladies European Tour in 2006.

The challenges

Considering the elevation changes and elevated tees, you'll have to be careful about club selection here. There are also plenty of strategically-placed lakes to avoid as you shoot towards large greens. Pro's tips: 'Play for position on the fairways and to the centre of the greens. The nape of the green plays an important part in how the ball will run to the hole.'

The resort experience

The resort buildings form a terracotta citadel with Moorish style that overlooks the Atlantic Ocean and the island of La Gomera from the slope of The Teide. The property stretches down to a private sandy beach that can be accessed by a cable car from the hotel's cliff-top perch. Lush vegetation and flowers flourish in the hotel grounds, thanks to the constant sunshine. The Ritz-Carlton features a spa with hydrotherapy pool and ten treatment rooms, seven swimming pools, 10 dining

Type of grasses: Fairways are Bermuda and greens are bentgrass.

When to play: 365 days a year – with little rain and warm conditions, this is the perfect climate for golf.

Par: 72

Yardage: 6,268 yards, or 6,281 metres

Slope: 136

Best hole: The signature hole is the par-5 10th (528 yards, 483 metres), which doglegs to the left and has out-of-bounds on both sides of the fairway. On the left side, there are three lakes running up to the green.

The pro says: 'To play well at Abama Golf, you have to exercise good course management. There are a lot of risk-and-reward holes.' – Brendan Breen options (including two Michelin star restaurants), and the Ritz Kids club with eco-minded activities for youngsters.

Dine and wine

With 10 dining options, you are spoiled for choice. However, I'll be putting two-Michelin-star M.B at the top of the list. Chef Martin Berasategui's signature restaurant serves Basque cuisine with authentic flavors. Next in line will be Japanese restaurant Kabuki, which has one Michelin star. The restaurants are blessed with fresh produce grown on Tenerife's fertile volcanic soil. You'll also find seafood (El Mirador), the 20/20 Steakhouse, Italian (Verona), traditional Spanish (Txoko), cocktails and light food (Beach House), buffet breakfast (La Veranda), Canary Island specialties (Los Chozos), light Clubhouse lunch (La Casa Club), beers on tap (Sports Bar), Cuban cocktails (Cubanika), and live music and more cocktails (Lobby Bar). There's also 24-hour room service should you get hungry in the wee hours.

The accommodation

The terracotta strikes a bold tone outside, but the interiors of the rooms are more mellow with softer tones and modern décor. These are spacious offerings, starting with the Deluxe Room (538 square feet, 50 square metres) with its furnished terrace and ocean, resort or golf course views. Floor-to-ceiling glass doors take advantage of the outlook as well. The bathroom has a double vanity, separate tub and toilet with bidet. It can sleep three adults, too. The Imperial Suite has an impressive 10,226 square feet (950 square metres) and includes a terrace with a heated swimming pool.

Other activities

Take the cable car to the summit of Mount Teide at 12,198 feet (3,718-metres), which is Spain's highest peak. You can also go paragliding with a professional, go whale-watching on a catamaran to the huge cliff of Los Gigantes, or throw yourself into any number of water sports, including jet-skis, kite surfing, surfing and parasailing.

ABOVE: Japanese restaurant Kabuki. *OPPOSITE: ABOVE:* El Mirador Swimming Pool; *MIDDLE:* Hotel room interior; *BELOW:* Poolside Lounging.

Sandy Hills course – The grand view on Hole No. 6.

Rosapenna

Rosapenna

Location: Rosapenna, Downings, Letterkenny, County Donegal, Ireland
Website: www.rosapenna.ie
Phone number: 00353 0 74 9155301

Located in County Donegal on the striking north-west coast of Ireland, the Rosapenna Hotel & Golf Resort is a haven for lovers of links golf. The 800-acre (324-hectare) dune system features two championship courses – Old Tom Morris links and Sandy Hills – as well as a nine-hole academy course and training facility. Old Tom Morris, the original course, was established after the four-time British Open Champion visited the region in 1891 and staked out a links course using the undulating landscape overlooking Tramore Beach at Sheephaven Bay. The Scotsman spread the word about the fresh links course back home and Rosapenna became a popular spot for some of the world's top golfers by the end of the 19th Century. A timber lodge was built to accommodate the travelling golfers, making this one of the oldest golf resorts in Ireland.

Old Tom Morris was redesigned and modernized in 2009 by Irishman Pat Ruddy of the European Club, replacing and separating the original back nine (known as the Coastguard Holes), which were then attached to a practice range. Sandy Hills, which was also designed by Ruddy, opened in 2003. It offers more length to challenge golfers, being about 300 yards (274 metres) longer than Old Tom Morris. The fairways run between the marram-covered dunes and there are elevated tees and greens. *Golf Digest Ireland* rated Sandy Hills as one of the best links courses in the country.

'A stunning modern links that funnels its way through centuries-old dunes created by, and still whipped by, the winds coming in off the Atlantic Ocean,' said Peter Acheson, *Golf Digest Ireland* editor*.

Considering the superb links challenge offered by both courses, *Planet Golf*'s Darius Oliver rates this as one of the best golf resorts in the country.

'It's a combination of a beautiful, out-of-the-way coastal location, two distinct links/dunes golf courses and the charming family-run hotel and hospitality business. You could easily spend a few days there, especially with good weather.'

The challenges
Try to keep on the fairways and out of the deep bunkers. Winds can whip up off the Atlantic Ocean to make scoring on both courses difficult. Keeping the ball low and using links techniques such as bump and running and putting off the green are recommended. Sandy Hills is the tougher challenge here.

ABOVE: Sandy Hills Course.

The resort experience

Rosapenna is a seasonal hotel but serves the golfers well during all but the winter months. The Casey family have owned and operated the resort since 1981, expanding the accommodation to a four-star 62-room hotel as well as the golf courses on offer. In 2012, they bought the nearby St. Patrick's Golf Links (which has been redesigned by Jack Nicklaus), adding 36 holes and some 370 acres (150 hectares) to the development. The resort features a spa that includes an indoor swimming pool, sauna and steam room. The Donegal coastline is a beautiful part of Ireland and well suited to links golf. Rosapenna's hotel and restaurant have grand views of Sheephaven Bay. The resort is about three and a half hours' drive from Dublin Airport and two hours' drive from Belfast International Airport.

Type of grasses: Both courses have a mix of fescue and bentgrass on the fairways and greens.

When to play: The courses open year-round, although the average temperatures drop to the single digit degrees Celsius during winter. The hotel is closed from November 1 to March 17.

Par: Old Tom Morris 71. Sandy Hills 72.

Yardage: Old Tom Morris 6,975 yards, 6,378 metres Sandy Hills 6,506 yards, 5,949 metres

Competition Scratch Score Rating: Old Tom Morris 71. Sandy Hills 72.

Best hole: The signature hole on Old Tom Morris Links is 14, a 198-yard (181-metre) par 3 with a bunker in front of a small green. On Sandy Hills, hole 6 (420-yard, 384-metre par 4), at the southern end of the course, a drive over a crest reveals a gorgeous view of beach and bay with Muckish Mountain in the backdrop.

The pro says: 'Both courses provide a stern links test while situated in one of the most beautiful bays in the world.' – Frank Casey Jnr, Director of Golf

Dine and wine

The Vardon Restaurant is named after English golfing legend Harry Vardon (with six Open titles), who had a hand in tweaking the Old Tom Morris course. No doubt Vardon would have enjoyed sitting down here for some of the fresh seafood that is delivered daily to the kitchen. Crab, shellfish, lobster and scallops are regularly on the menu. It's a great spot to watch the sunset over Sheephaven Bay, too.

After dinner, enjoy a single malt Irish whiskey at the James Braid Bar (named after another Open champion who helped renovate the original course).

The accommodation

The rooms are elegant and comfortable. They start with a Classic Room (300 square feet, 28 square metres) with the basics (double bed, refrigerator, en suite bathroom) and step up to the Bayview Suite (450 square feet, 42 square metres) with king-size bed, private balcony and more luxurious bathrooms. All rooms come with Wi-Fi but you'll probably be too busy enjoying the views over Sheephaven Bay to connect.

Other activities

Take a copy of the *Sheephaven Bay Walking Guide* from reception and enjoy one of the great walks along the coastline here. The beautiful Glenveagh National Park is a 15-minute drive from the hotel, too. In the summer, you can also enroll in surf school and paddle out into the Atlantic at one of Donegal's beautiful sandy beaches. Horse riding, deep-sea fishing and scuba diving can all be easily organized as well.

*Source: www.rosapenna.ie/sandy-hills-links.html#.WL1VpvmGMRk

ABOVE: Old Tom Morris course.

OPPOSITE ABOVE: Rosapenna Hotel; *MIDDLE:* Room view; *BELOW:* Rosapenna Hotel Exterior.

Rosewood
Tucker's Point

Hamilton Parish, Bermuda

Rosewood Tucker's Point

Location: 60 Tucker's Point Dr., Hamilton Parish, HS 02 Bermuda
Website: rosewoodhotels.com/en/bermuda/experiences/active-leisure/golf
Phone number: 1 441 298 4000

The island of Bermuda lies approximately 665 miles (1,070 kilometres) off the east coast of the United States in the Atlantic Ocean. In 2017, the British Overseas Territory hosted the 35th America's Cup in the famous Great Sound, which sits on the west side of the archipelago. Rosewood Tucker's Point resort is located on the north-east side of the island, only about 2.8 miles (4.5 kilometres) away from LF Wade International Airport. The Tucker's Point Golf Club, a grand building positioned on a hilltop, is part of the resort community here and guests are welcome – they'll find a complimentary day locker for your gear.

Bermuda is known as 'the Jewel of the Atlantic', and the Tucker's Point golf course proves it is a small jewel in a very large ocean. From some higher spots, you can see both ends of the island. Large elevation changes on the layout are the key feature of this course, which was redesigned by American Robert Rulewich in 2002. He took a layout that was originally designed by Charles H. Banks in 1932 and embraced the hilly terrain that overlooks Castle Harbour to the north, Harrington Sound to the west and the Atlantic Ocean to the east. The course boasts of beautiful coastal views.

Elevated tees, undulating fairways, links-style holes and slick TifEagle greens make this a fun but not overbearing challenge. However, the great elevation changes mean you must be careful which club you choose for each shot. According to Jack Bridges, First Golf Professional at Rosewood Tucker's Point: 'The golf course has extreme elevation changes that move naturally with the landscape,' Bridges said. 'Robert Rulewich is the former chief designer for Robert Trent Jones. His biggest challenge was laying a course over such hilly terrain. It's a great golf course that provides a challenge, but won't beat up the mid- to-high handicapper.'

'In terms of playability, the large elevation changes on almost every shot sets it apart from most other golf courses in the world. Elevation changes here can account for a three-club difference in some places.'

Golf carts equipped with GPS course guides will help you traverse the hills and give you distances to greens and hazards.

Opposite page *AND OVERLEAF:* Tucker's Point Beach Club.

The challenges

Elevation changes and varying wind conditions off the Atlantic can make club selection difficult. The pro's tips: 'Favor being on the fairway over distance. The rough can get very thick and the ball will always sit down. Past the rough there is dense vegetation; hit your ball in there and you won't retrieve it. When it's breezy, swing easy!'

The resort experience

Rosewood Tucker's Point is a highly-recognized luxury resort, having earned the AAA Four Diamond Award, *Forbes Travel Guide – Four-Star Resort*, and *Golf Magazine's Editors' Choice Award for Best Resorts of The Americas* all in 2016. There are 88 suites and guest rooms with bright interiors and classic décor that suits the British seaside colony.

Type of grasses: Fairways of Bermuda grass and on the greens TifEagle, a Bermuda hybrid that makes for a quick putting surface.

When to play: Open year-round. The perfect months are May/June and October/November, although the average monthly temperatures are just fine throughout.

Par: 70

Yardage: 6,200 yards, 5,669 metres

Slope: 124

Rating: 69.5

Best hole: Hole 17 is a drivable par 4 with about 315 yards (288 metres) to make it on the green after a slight dogleg left. The elevated tee box provides a stunning view of Castle Harbour.

The pro says: 'The large elevation changes on almost every shot sets Tucker's Point apart from most other golf courses in the world. Match this with some of the strong ocean breezes that we get and you are in for an interesting game!'
– Jack Bridges, First Golf Professional

The resort has two swimming pools to bathe your blues away. The Castle Harbour Pool has a lap lane as well as private alcoves when you want a break. The Palm Court Pool overlooks a sunken grotto known as Coffee Chine. The chaise lounges and private cabanas are perfect for kicking back in. Snacks and drinks can be ordered alongside both pools.

Sense Spa will help your body's rejuvenation on this visit to Bermuda. From massages to manicures, expect to be pampered at this Rosewood facility. The Sense of Bermuda Experience is a signature service – over 4.5 hours you receive a Cedar Warming Massage, facial, manicure and pedicure, followed by fresh lunch.

The resort is about five hours' flight from the east coast of the US, but a short drive from the airport.

Dine and wine

After golf, you have two sound options right in the club house. You can enjoy a steak in the Grill Room or sit down for authentic Italian at Sul Verde as you watch over Castle Harbour. Back at the hotel, you can book a table for breakfast or dinner at The Point. This signature restaurant features 80-foot-long (24-metre-long) murals that depict eight seaports on its walls. The menu highlights include grilled local swordfish with neck clams and Wadson Farm chicken breast stuffed with pine nuts and chanterelles. I'll be trying a five-course tasting menu (you can pick 'Land' or 'Sea').

Within the Point Restaurant, slip into the Wine Room, which features some 3,000 bottles on display. You can choose a candlelit dinner here, too. The Chef's

Table sounds like a fun experience, dining in the kitchen next to Executive Chef Gerry Adam. Then there is Tucker's Bar for drinks with views of Harrington Sound, Sur Mer – the Beach Club Restaurant that sits by a pink-sand beach as well as the Beach Club's Bar, which will serve you poolside or at the beach.

The accommodation
Even the basic guest rooms have fine coastal views of Castle Harbour or Harrington Sound. The Manor House Superior Room (500 square feet, 46 square metres) features a balcony, walk-in showers, separate bathtub, and dual vanities. Bathrobes and slippers are provided as well as plush Italian linens. At the other end of the scale, the Walsingham Suite (1,650 square feet, 153 square metres) has a dining area with wet bar, living area with a fireplace and a half-bath for guests. The king-size bed and en suite bathroom you'd expect.

Other activities
Before indulging at the Sense Spa, you may want to earn your treatment in the 1,900-square-foot (176-square-metre) fitness centre, which has a lawn for yoga and Tai Chi. You'll find four clay tennis courts and pros ready to sharpen your game, as well as a croquet lawn, too. But I'm really interested in the water sports here. The Dive & Watersports Centre will sign you up for a diving adventure aboard the Tidal Pull, a 31-foot (9-metre) dive boat that takes you out to explore untouched coral reefs, caves and other dive sites in the pristine waters. Deep-sea fishing expeditions, windsurfing, and Kruger and Laser sailing boats are also available.

ABOVE: Manor House Suite Terrace; BELOW: Spa Reflecting Pool.
OPPOSITE ABOVE: Shower Room; BELOW: Tucker's Point Beach.

Sonnenalp Golf Course.

Sonnenalp/
Oberallgäu

Ofterschwang, Bavaria, Germany

Sonnenalp/Oberallgäu

Location: Sonnenalp 1, 87527 Ofterschwang, Germany
Website: sonnenalp.de/golf
Phone number: 08 321 272 181

Set in the Bavarian mountains in the south of Germany not far from the principality of Liechtenstein, this resort features two fine 18-hole courses. You'll enjoy stunning Alpine views as you progress through a layout that keeps surprising.

'The routing must be considered a stroke of genius due to the dearth of contiguous space,' writes Ulrich Mayring for Top100golfcourses.com. 'More than once it looks like the golfer has finally played himself into a dead-end, but the course keeps on winding its way forward between houses, barns, pastures, ravines and mountains.'

Sonnenalp has a flatter layout through meadows and forests but is still worth playing. The snow-capped Allgäu Alps add a scenic backdrop and you can stop at a rustic Halfway House before the 10th hole for refreshments.

On Sonnenalp, golfers will be challenged by doglegs, ponds, small streams, strategically-placed bunkers and undulating greens.

The five-star hotel on site also offers its guests weekly tournaments to sign up for, introducing an element of competition to the beautiful setting. You can also warm up on the nine-hole Gundelsberg course.

Owner Karlheinz Fäßler employed Swiss golf course architect Donald Harradine to design Sonnenalp in 1975, whilst local designer Kurt Rossknecht completed Oberallgäu and Gundelsberg in 2004, establishing this resort as one of Europe's top golfing destinations. Rossknecht modernized Sonnenalp in 2008.

There are two clubhouses – Waldhaus and Seehaus – with accompanying pro shops servicing golfers here, too. The clubhouses each have golf academies that employ the latest teaching methods, such as video feedback and sports psychology, to help sharpen your game.

The challenges
After the driveable par-4 1st hole on Oberallgäu, smart club selection is needed to stay out of trouble from bunkers, lakes and trees on this windy, mountainous course.

The resort experience
Expect five-star service at the Sonnenalp Hotel, a resort that started operations as a lodge in 1919 by Ludwig and Resi Fässler. The property has stayed in the family for four generations (currently managed by Anna-Maria and Michael Fäßler) and aims to bring that family warmth to its service. The spa and wellness centre is set out over 107,639 square feet (10,000 square metres) with ample facilities.

ABOVE: Oberallgäu Golf Course.

With three bars, multiple lounges, two libraries and a concert room that features bands playing everything from jazz to Bavarian folk for guests, the resort offers plenty of places to relax.

It also has the world's best whirlpool, according to Ulrich Mayring: 'The destination offers anything you expect from a top mountain resort.'

Sonnenalp Hotel won the Diners Club Award for European Resort of the Year in 2012 and TopHotel Award – 'Edutainment' in 2016 for its educational and entertaining activities for children (see activities) amongst many other plaudits.

Type of grasses: The fairways are Poa supina turf, and the greens Penn A-4 creeping bentgrass.

When to play: March – November. This becomes an Alpine ski resort when the snow starts falling in winter.

Par: Sonnenalp par 73; Oberallgäu par 72

Yardage: Sonnenalp 6,707 yards, 6,133 metres Oberallgäu 6,492 yards, 5,936 metres

Slope: Sonnenalp 136. Oberallgäu 127

Rating: Sonnenalp 74.8. Oberallgäu 71.5

The manager says: On Sonnenalp: 'The ambitious golfer will be challenged by doglegs, ingrown ponds, small streams, bunkers and tricky greens that need technical skill, while the less ambitious golfer can enjoy the fair course at the same time.'

On Oberallgäu: 'The championship course was designed by the renowned golf course architect Kurt Rossknecht. A round of golf here, with a breathtaking 360 degree panoramic view, is a special experience. Oberallgäu is set against the picturesque scenery of the Nebelhorn and is considered one of the most charming Alpine courses in Germany. The fairways are harmoniously integrated into the beautiful landscape with its old stock of trees. The undulating fairways are indeed challenging.'

– Hanspeter Schratt, Manager of the Golf Resort Sonnenalp-Oberallgäu

Dine and wine

The Sonnenalp's Michelin-star restaurant Silberdistel is located at the top of the main building. Enjoy great views of the Allgäu Mountains as you dine on nine courses of gourmet food. The main dining restaurant in the centre of the building is good for breakfast and buffet lunch. Or you can opt for barbecue, steaks and burgers at Fäßlers Grillstube.

The Waldhaus and Seehaus clubhouses each feature a restaurant you can settle into after a round. The former has a classic wooded Alpine lodge feel, while the latter is built in an Allgäu country-house style. The chefs use local produce to prepare Bavarian and German dishes. Watch out for the cakes, which are baked on site, and enjoy the Alpine view as you dig in. There's also a day restaurant in the spa called Seepferdl where you can eat light meals in your bathrobe.

The accommodation

Seven different room types are on offer – 218 in total – to match your budget and the size of your group. It starts with the compact EZ Comfort and Deluxe for single travellers happy to fit into 140 square feet (13 square metres). There is a modern and fresh look about these rooms. At the other end of the scale, you can retire to your own Alpine chalet. Within the 1,528 square feet (142 square metres) on offer you'll find two bedrooms, a luxury bathroom and a fire place to cozy up to. These Berghirsch apartments are dog-friendly to the point of having a dog mini-bar with treats. Woof!

Best hole: Oberallgäu's 'Pond Witch', the par-4 4th hole, offers two truly challenging shots to reach a small target in regulation. Avoid the trees on the left off the tee but make sure you don't cut the ball into the lake on the right, which follows the dogleg to the right all the way to the green. Then on Hole 7, a par 4 dubbed 'Grand Canyon' will see you hitting downhill over canyon and water hazard. On Sonnenalp's 'Halfway House', the par-4 10th, golfers will face a stream to hit over, and a fairway that narrows on both sides with trees closing in. If you make it past that, your approach shot will have to carry a pond on the left side in front of the green, which is also flanked by two bunkers. Hole 13, a par 3 called 'S'Insele', is another top challenge with the green almost surrounded by water.

Other activities

The spa and wellness centre provides everything from anti-aging cosmetic treatments and massages for couples to physiotherapy and traditional Ayurveda treatments. But Sonnenalp's differentiating strength is its focus on keeping kids happy during the German holiday season. There are over 70 activities for children of all ages to throw themselves into – many aim to educate youngsters about sustainability, wildlife and the environment. They might enjoy horse-riding, water-skiing, canyoning, ziplining up to 75 mph (120 km/h) down the Alpspitzkick, ballooning over the mountains, and even tandem paragliding! Then the little people can chill out in the children's cinema or take a theatre workshop after that. How completely cool.

OPPOSITE: Indoor Pool; *ABOVE:* View from Deluxe Double Room; *BELOW:* Dining Veranda.

South Cape Owners' Club
Golf course – Hole No. 16.

South Cape
Owners' Club

Gyeongsangnam-do, South Korea

South Cape Owners' Club

Location: 41 Jindong-ri, Changseon-myeon, Namhae, Gyeongsangnam-do, South Korea
website: www.southcape.co.kr/main.asp
Phone number: 82 1644 0280

Frequently billed as the South Korea's premier golf resort by golf experts, South Cape features a championship 18-hole course that sits on the beautiful Namhae Island, off the south-east coast of the country. The layout, which was designed by American Kyle Phillips and completed in 2013, makes full use of its position overlooking the Korea Strait to deliver fairways that play to the edge of rugged cliff tops above the water. Phillips describes it as having a links feel without being a links landscape.

'It is simply an amazing coastline,' Phillips said *. 'Every hole has a view of the sea, which comes into play on eight holes. It is one of the most striking coastlines in golf.'

There are plenty of elevation changes as you try to keep the ball on the beautifully manicured fairways and undulating greens.

'The most memorable stretch of holes on the card begins with the downhill par 5 11th and carries on for half a dozen holes, highlighted by a stunning pair of waterside par 3s at the 149-yard (136-metre) 14th and the 223-yard (204-metre) 16th holes,' writes Wuhyeok Jeon for 100TopGolfCourses.com, which rated it as the No. 1 course in South Korea in 2017.

These waterside par 3s have been compared to Pebble Beach's famous Hole 7 and Cyprus Point's Hole 16, respectively.

The clubhouse itself is an outstanding, and chic, architectural design, built into the side of a mountain. In fact, everything about this development, which was the brainchild of South Korean entrepreneur Jae Bong Chung, is stylish.

BELOW: South Cape Owners' Club from above,
OPPOSITE: South Cape Owners' Club Golf course – Hole No. 14

The challenges

You'll be hitting across valleys and the ocean on various holes, which will make some nervous. However, the wide fairways provide comfort on the elevated tees.

The resort experience

South Korean golf journalist Hwa Young Nam rated this the best resort in the country, and it is a most impressive development. The course was built as an exclusive club for owners of 130 sea villas, but it is open to guests of the South Cape Spa & Suite. This luxury boutique hotel has 49 suites along the shoreline and 10 cliff houses facing the ocean, and subsequently the views of the coastline are outstanding. Billing itself as 'the world's most artistic healing place', this resort aims to give you a peaceful break away from the usual noise of the world. The interiors feature furniture and fixtures by well-known artists, giving visitors the feeling they are in an art gallery rather than a swanky hotel.

Type of grasses: Kentucky Blue fairways, T1 Bentgrass greens and fescue rough.

When to play: Year-round.

Par: 72

Yardage: 7,313 yards, 6,685 metres

Slope: 138

Rating: 75.2

Best hole: The 223 yard (204-metre) 16th hole is a stunning par 3 where you hit down to a green almost surrounded by sea cliffs and guarded by four giant bunkers.

The designer says: 'There is a good variety of strategy through the course,' said Kyle Phillips*, whose stylish bunkering replicates the natural outline of the island coast. 'You can play bump-and-run shots, or you can be aggressive. There are multiple lines of play, depending on how you want to attack the golf course.'

Chill out to vinyl records in the music library, have a swim in the long infinity pool, sample a rare vintage in the wine bar, or sweat away the toxins in the sauna – just relax.

Dine and wine

You can enjoy both Korean and Western food here but I'd be choosing the seafood. The thrust of South Cape's restaurant is to 'maximize taste of the local and seasonal raw integrant' in keeping with the seaside location. And the view from here is stunning.

The accommodation

The bunker-like design of the hotel rooms may be striking from the exterior but the interior is luxurious and stylish. The four-room cliff-houses feature four rooms with about 6,458 square feet (600 square metres) of space.

Other activities

There are two seaside trekking paths – a 2-hour and 1.5-hour course – that you are invited to walk barefoot. However, I think I'll be heading to the spa, which is managed by an anti-aging therapy group known as Chaum, for a Korean massage.

*Source: kylephillips.com

ABOVE: Infinity pool and wine bar.

OPPOSITE ABOVE: Infinity pool; *MIDDLE:* Restaurant interior; *BELOW:* The Cliff house.

The Kittocks Course – Hole No. 2.

St Andrews,
Fairmont

St Andrews, Fairmont

Location: A917, St Andrews KY16 8PN, Scotland, UK

Website: www.fairmont.com/st-andrews-scotland ; www.theexperiencestandrews.com

Phone number: 1 44 1334 837000 ; 1 866 840 8208

St Andrews is known as 'the home of golf' and is full of a sporting history that makes visiting the ancient town on Scotland's east coast, in county Fife, seem like a pilgrimage for golfers. Golf has been played over the links of St Andrews for over 600 years. It is the original links course. From King David I's charter in 1123 marking it common land belonging to the townspeople, to Archbishop Hamilton's charter in 1552 recognizing the locals' right to play on the links, to the 1764 transition from a 22- to 18-hole layout, through to American great Bobby Jones famously defending the Open Championship's Claret Jug in 1927, it has a truly rich history.

The Old Course (par 72, 6,721 yards or 6,146 metres) is a must-play, with its iconic features such as the Swilcan Bridge and 10-foot deep Hell Bunker on the par-5 14th hole, which has destroyed many a round including one by Jack Nicklaus, who recorded a 10 in the 1995 Open Championship. There are seven large double greens to hit onto, as well as 112 individually-named bunkers to avoid.

Since its development in the late 1990s, Fairmont St Andrews has become a popular destination for golfers to stay at when they come to lap up the history and play the Old Course. It also has two fine courses to play. The Kittocks and Torrance courses combine traditional Scottish links play with modern golf architecture. The courses overlook the town of St Andrews, including the historic castle and university, and the Scottish coastline and North Sea. European golf writer Jo Maes summed up the two layouts after recommending the resort.

'The Kittocks, which translates as feisty lady, is named after the ravine running through the course where a family of local deer resides. It's a course that plays along the Fife coastline with unparalleled views across the bay and even as far away as Carnoustie and the coastal town of Arbroath. The Torrance—designed by former Ryder Cup captain, Scottish golfer Sam Torrance—is the more challenging of the two, resembling a Scottish links with revetted bunkers and large greens.'

Torrance worked with the Americans Denis Griffiths and the late Gene Sarazen to come up with a challenging 7,230-yard (6,611-metre) layout that finishes on the coastal cliff tops. Fairway bunkers and traps around the green can be punishing, and watch out for water hazards on holes 1, 3, 14.

The Torrance Course hosted the Scottish Seniors Open between 2009 and 2014 and was the Open Championship qualifying course in 2010.

OPPOSITE: The golf courses at St Andrews Fairmont overlook the North Sea.

The Kittocks Course was designed by Sarazen, Griffiths and Australian Bruce Devlin and opened in 2002. Golfers will find double greens and deep pot bunkers, and some of the most beautiful coastal views in golf along the way, especially on holes 7 and 15, which has a cliff-top green. Amy Yates wrote on Top100GolfCourse.com:

'You'll need to be either an exceptionally good player or a masochist to play this par-72 course from the back tees (7,192 yards, 6,576 metres).'

The challenges

On the Old Course, avoid the deep pot-holed bunkers such as the Spectacles on the 5th and Hell Bunker on the 14th and bring your best links game to get the ball near the flags on the double greens. On the Fairmont courses, pot-holed bunkers, water hazards that include a stream and two lakes, and large undulating greens make both courses tough links challenges, especially from the back tees. Pro's tips: select the appropriate tee and control your shot to avoid being out-of-bounds on a beach or hacking the ball in deep rough, and 'as with all Scottish sea-side courses, try to set yourself the goal of never going in a bunker.'

Type of grasses: The Old Course has a mix of bentgrass and fescue throughout *. On both Fairmont courses, the fairways are ryegrass, and greens are a mix of bentgrass and fescue.

When to play: The golf courses are open 12 months of the year but will close with severe frost or snow in December through to February.

Par: All courses 72

Slope / Standard Scratch Score / Yardage:
Old Course 73.1 / 132 / 6,721 yards or 6,146 metres
Torrance Course 138 / 75 / 7,230 yards, 6,611 metres

Kittocks Course 136 / 75 / 7,192 yards, 6,576 metres **

The pro says: 'I fell in love with it the first day I played it. There's just no other golf course that is even remotely close.' – Jack Nicklaus on The Old Course**

'Both golf courses offer a challenge to every level of player due to the player having the choice of four teeing areas. Every hole has breathtaking sea views. There are large, smooth and subtly undulating greens and generous fairways with deep, revetted bunkering.' – John Kerr, PGA professional, Fairmont St Andrews

The resort experience
This is one of the United Kingdom's most outstanding resorts. It was awarded Best Large Hotel of the Year 2015 (Scottish Golf Tourism Awards), European Resort of the Year 2012 (International Association Golf Tour Operators) and International Resort Hotel of the Year in 2009 (Scottish Hotel of the Year Awards). This five-star hotel can cater for everything from large conferences – it hosted a G20 summit in 2009 — through to golfing parties and honeymooners.

The resort is set out on 520-acres (210 hectares) of land overlooking the town of St. Andrews across the bay, including the castle and university, as well as the North Sea. The beige and blue buildings have a quaint European look to them, but the interiors are both modern and elegant. The spa features an indoor pool, sauna, steam room, jacuzzi, fitness centre and 12 treatment rooms.

'This is a big hotel and conference centre where many of the professionals stay when playing the Open and the Dunhill Links,' said Jo Maes. 'Like everywhere in Scotland, the atmosphere is cozy, and with the staff dressed in local tartan, it has that sense of Scottish heritage.'

It's also a good base to use to go and play some of the other fabulous courses in the area including Kingsbarns, Crail, Lundin, and Leven. Those who want to stay closer to the Old Course should consider the five-star Old Course Hotel (www.oldcoursehotel. co.uk).

Dine and wine
There are six restaurants or eateries to choose from. The Squire will take care of your buffet breakfast with some extravagant local touches (I might pass on the Haggis!). St Andrews Bar & Grill has a SABG Signature Burger that you can consume as you look out over the golf courses and cliff tops – the outdoor deck is a good spot for watching sunsets. You can also pick out fresh seafood, such as a lobster from the tank, and pair it with a Josper-grilled steak – Scottish Surf and Turf.

Otherwise head to the Rock and Spindle family bar (pool tables and board games available) for a craft beer or single-malt whiskey. Kittocks Den has coffee and a juice bar that makes smoothies to order, while the Atrium Lounge is good for afternoon tea with scones and jam, pastries, cakes and sandwiches.

The accommodation
Fairmont St Andrews has four types of guest rooms, five suite options and manor homes to choose from. The interiors are elegant, décor luxurious and amenities five star. The king-sized beds have thick duvet covers while the floor-to-ceiling windows provide plenty of natural light plus great views of the Tay Estuary and North Sea. An Atrium Room (237 square feet, 22 square metres) does not come with the sea view, but does have a king-size bed plus a walk-in shower and tub. Or you could go with a Kingdom of the Fife suite (1,518 square feet, 141 square metres), which

OPPOSITE: The Kittocks Course plays out to a peninsula.

has a living room with fireplace, a bedroom with two dressing rooms attached and a separate Jacuzzi bathroom and shower room. The balcony has great views of the courses, coastline and St Andrews.

Other activities

Hire a bike from the resort and explore the local area, send the teenager to Teenzone to chill out on bean bags and play games consoles or air hockey, or hike the Fife Coastal Path, which goes from Culross to St Andrews and on to the Tay Bridge. The walk has some great views of the coastline and you may want to stop off at the ruins of St Andrews Castle for some local history.

*Source: www.europeantour.com/europeantour/season=2011/tournamentid=2011071/venue/

**Source: www.standrewsgolf.com/golf-courses/old-course.htm

***Source: www.standrews.com/Play/Courses/Old-course

Best hole: On the Old Course, hole 17 – dubbed 'Road' – is one of the best non-water holes in the golf due to the risk-reward, angles, safe routes and dangers on the 455-yard (416-metre) par 4, according to US writer Bob Fagan. The 618-yard (565-metre) hole 14 is the longest hole on the course and also has the famous Hell Bunker to avoid in the middle of the fairway. On the Torrance course, hole 16 (429-yard, par 4) hits downhill towards the sea with an exceptional view over St Andrews Bay. There is a challenging approach shot to a cliff-top green that has a 100-foot (30-metre) drop off the back edge to the beach. Don't pick too much club here! On Kittocks, the 17th hole (502-yard, par 4) plays along the cliff top with the beach flanking the entire right side of the hole. A forced carry to a huge cliff-top green awaits the bravest (or foolhardy) golfers on approach in regulation.

Family pool and Altamira
Cantina Gourmet Restaurant.

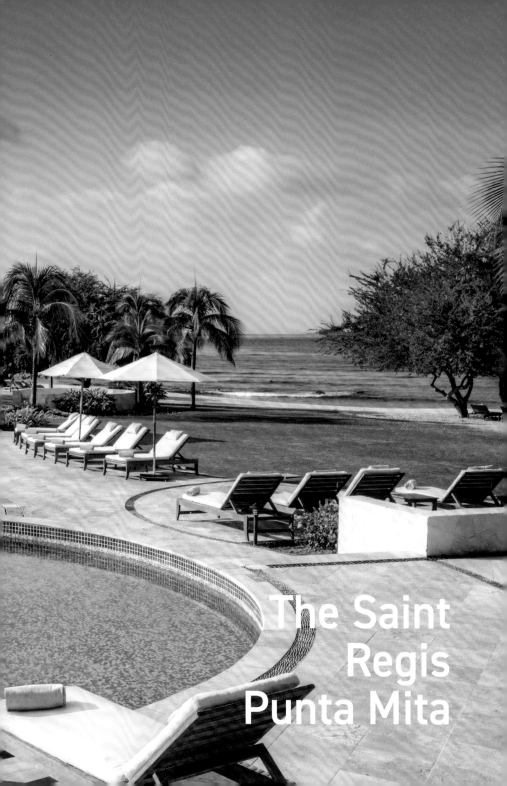

The Saint Regis Punta Mita

Nayarit, Mexico

The Saint Regis Punta Mita

Location: Lote H-4, Carretera Federal 200, km 19.5, Punta de Mita, Nayarit, 63734, Mexico

Website: www.stregispuntamita.com

Phone number: 52 329 291 5800

There is something about turquoise waters and sandy beaches that puts me instantly at ease. It might just help my swing here at The Saint Regis Punta Mita, which sits next to the quaint fishing village of Riveria Nayarit in the middle of Mexico's Pacific Coast. After a 45-minute drive from Puerto Vallarta International Airport, you'll be able to tee off at one of two courses designed by Jack Nicklaus: Punta Mita Pacifico, which has eight holes next to the Pacific Ocean or Banderas Bay, and Punta Mita Bahia, which has water features and lakes spread throughout its undulating fairways.

Pacifico is the signature course here and it boasts a novelty hole (3B) dubbed 'The Tail of the Whale,' the world's only natural island green. It's optional, but you're surely going to play this one. You need to carry the ball over 170 yards (155 metres) of the Pacific Ocean (it plays up to 194 yards / 177 metres) before hopping in an amphibious vehicle that will take you to the green (provided the conditions aren't too rough, according to *Golf Digest*). The green is surrounded by rocks and sand traps.

It's not uncommon to spot humpback whales during their migration between December and March during a round at Pacifico. On the landlocked side of the course, there are gorgeous views of the Sierra Madre Mountains.

Bahia's 18th hole plays down to one of Mexico's best surfing spots – the El Faro break. It's a 571-yard (522-metre) par 5 that reminds you that it's time to get wet as soon as you put your clubs away.

The challenges

Punta Mita Pacifico: the greens and fairways are generous, but avoid the deep bunkers and odd palm trees and try not to spray the ball into the Pacific.

Punta Mita Bahia: some well-positioned bunkers and plenty of water hazards to avoid here as well as undulating greens and fairways to deal with.

The resort experience

There are in fact two resorts that give you access to the golf courses – Saint Regis and Four Seasons (fourseasons.com/puntamita, +52 329 291 60000). Saint Regis Punta

OPPOSITE: Pacifico's Tail of the Whale.

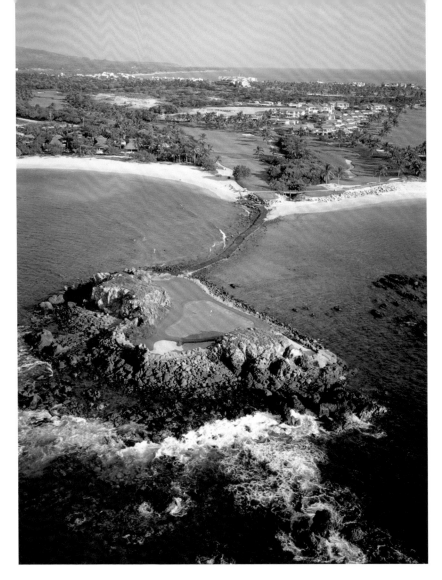

Type of grasses: Pacifico's greens use Champion turf while Bahia has Min Verde turf. Tees, fairways and roughs on both courses use 419 Bermuda grass.

When to play: Year-round at this tropical retreat.

Par: Pacifico 72, Bahia 72

Yardage: Pacifico 7,001 yards, 6,402 metres (or 7,014 yards, 6,414 metres with optional hole.) Bahia 7,035 yards, 6,433 metres

Slope: Pacifico 131, Bahia 135

Rating: Pacifico 72.7 (or 72.9 with optional hole), Bahia 74

Best hole: Pacifico – hole 3B, a par 3 dubbed 'The Tail of the Whale' that is an island green with a 170-yard (155-metre) carry over the ocean. Bahia – the 571-yard (522-metre) hole 18, which plays down to the El Faro surf break.

Mita has been recommended by renowned American golf writer Bob Fagan, while Canadian golf journalist Dave Finn rates Four Seasons among the 10 best resorts he has stayed at. Both esteemed golf writers have travelled to hundreds of resorts across the world.

Both are top options to stay at but I will opt for the newer Saint Regis here. It was recognized by the World Golf Awards as 'Latin America's Best Golf Hotel' and 'Mexico's Best Golf Hotel' in 2016. This is five-star luxury right next to a stunning surf beach. There are 120 rooms, suites and villas to choose from on 22-acres (9 hectares) of manicured grounds, which feature palms, lawns and flowers and three outdoor pools (beachside, family and adult). The Mediterranean-inspired architecture of the dwellings suits the tropical setting.

Regis guests enjoy rituals such as champagne sabering (opening a magnum with a sword), afternoon tea, the Mita Mary ritual (made with tequila, not vodka) or choosing the catch of the day from local fisherman with the chef.

Dine and wine

There are five restaurants to choose from, including the signature eatery Carolina. The AAA-Five-Diamond restaurant specializes in modern Mexican cuisine made with regional and local fare, such as pozole verde ceviche or suckling pig. Wines are paired, naturally, as you sit on the terrace and enjoy the ocean views. Other restaurant options include Sea Breeze (beach-side grill), Las Marietas Restaurant and Bar (traditional Mexican), Altamira Cantina Gourmet (Mexican food and craft

ABOVE: Pacifico's Hole No 18. meets coastline, Hotel Gardens, Dining Area.

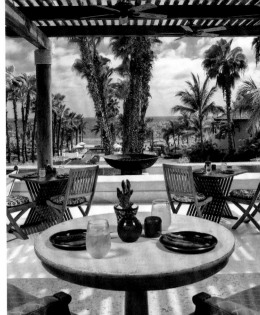

beer) and Mita Mary Boat Bar & Bistro (fresh fish). Tequila is made in the nearby Puerto Vallarta area and is in ample supply once you've reached the 19th hole.

The accommodation
Comfortable and private lodgings start with a 600- to 640-foot-square (56- to 59-square-metre) Deluxe Room for two with king-size bed (features terrace, outdoor shower, in-room movie system, a sun bed and Wi-Fi) through to the three-bedroom Presidential Villa (two kings, two single beds) for up to six guests with 3,100 square feet (288 square metres). Here you can enjoy your own terrace with pool, jacuzzi and outdoor shower, plus a dining-room inside.

Other activities
There is plenty to do at and around the resort. Every month they celebrate a Full Moon Party at St Regis, which sounds intriguing. Or perhaps learn how to make guacamole from scratch, or how to create a Mexican cocktail. To earn your massage at Remeda Spa you should probably take a salsa lesson, play tennis or sign up for a bike tour. And the Children's Club features piñata making, treasure hunts and a painting lesson.

However, the open water is calling me here. Punta Mita is a top scuba diving location so I'll be exploring the nearby Marietas Islands Marine Reserve. You can hire a yacht, surf, snorkel and, between December and April, go whale watching, too.

LEFT: Hotel Gardens; *RIGHT:* Dining Area.

Hotel and courses from above.

St. Wendel

Saarland, Germany

St. Wendel

Location: Golfparkallee 1, 66606 St. Wendel, Germany
Website: golf-absolute.de/stwendel ; angelshotel-golfpark.de
Phone number: 0 68 51 97 98 00

Located near Germany's western border with France, St. Wendel is a golf destination that features a 27-hole championship layout and a nine-hole par-3 course on a 370-acre (150-hectare) site. Naturally, the focus is on the former three-by-nine-hole combination. Holes 1, 9, 10, 18, 19 and 27 arrive or depart from the clubhouse, making it easy to divide your round up. The view from the clubhouse is something to behold, too, taking in courses that are set out over hills, thick forest and lakes.

St. Wendelinus, after whom the town is named, is the Patron Saint of herdsman and country people, so he may not be the best holy person to pray to to keep your scoring low here. And your game will be tested on this course, which was designed by Wolfgang Jersombeck.

'The 27 holes offer some of the most boisterous golf I've played,' said German golf writer Ulrich Mayring. 'The excitement just never stops – every hole is a complete thrill. St. Wendel is a great retreat in the summer heat because it is at a bit of an altitude.'

The challenges
You'll find trouble of all sorts off the tee unless you control your ball. There are both green-side and fairway bunkers to contend with, plus holes where you'll have to fly the ball over water.

The resort experience
Angel's Hotel is a modern building with four-star services throughout its 46 rooms. The designers gave attention to using low-allergy materials in items such as comforters and pillows. The bathrooms feature natural stone with a shower or tub. Each room comes with a spectacular view.

Dine and wine
St Wendel's restaurant offers fine gourmet dining. Mains include a glazed duck breast served with onion vanilla confit and nutty potato purée as well as a homemade pasta with tarragon, peas, garlic and bacon. Then finish off with an apple strudel with ice cream and vanilla sauce. You will also find a bistro menu with quicker meals such as burgers and schnitzels. The breakfast is included in your room fee.

St. Wendels Golf Courses.

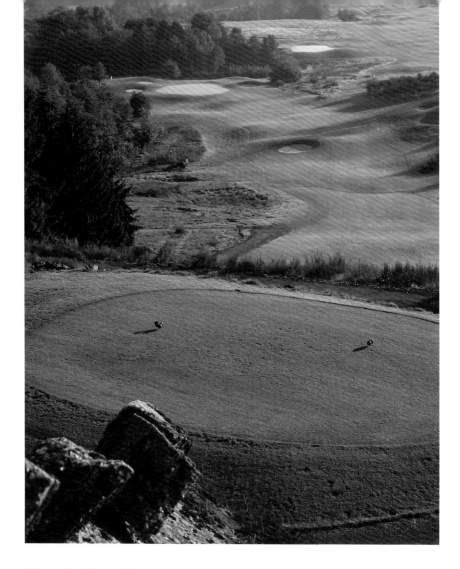

When to play: Try to visit during the dryer months, April through to September. The course can quickly become unplayable in wet conditions, according to Ulrich Mayring. November is the wettest month.

Par: Three combinations of two nine-hole courses to make up par 72.

Yardage: Course A+B 6,570 yards, 6,008 metres; Course C+A 6,827 yards, 6,243 metres; Course B+C 6,851 yards, 6,265 metres.

Slope: Course A+B 135; Course C+A 138; Course B+C 137

Rating: Course A+B 72.2; Course C+A 73.4; Course B+C 73.7

Best hole: Hole 9 on course A has a nasty fairway bunker on the right side before the dogleg left. Another long bunker sits in front of the green as well as a lake directly in front of the putting surface, testing your distance control.

The accommodation

Modern and chic hotel rooms that are designed for singles or couples.

Other activities

The resort is geared towards golfers, but the wellness and relaxation centre has 14 packages to pamper yourself or your partner. 'Warm-hearted' is a fine choice – you get full-body exfoliation, a bath in a luxury tub, followed by a hot-stone massage. If you are feeling more adventurous, try one of the many hiking trails around St Wendel and the Saar-Hunsrück nature park, or take the children to the nearby Gondwana Dinosaur Park, which is fantastic.

ABOVE: Sunrise on the green; *BELOW:* Sauna, Hotel Bar.
OPPOSITE ABOVE: Lake beside Hotel; *BELOW:* Hotel Exterior.

Gary Player Course – Hole No. 16.

Sun City

North West Province, South Africa

Sun City

Location: 0316 Rustenburg, North West Province, South Africa
Website: go2africa.com/destinations/sun-city/why-go
suninternational.com/sun-city/
Phone number: 27 11 780 7000

With the motto 'A World Within a City,' you would expect this to be a big development with a lot to offer and frankly it is a huge resort. As Ernie Els expressed to me when recommending it as one of his favorite resorts in the world: 'Sun City is an incredible place; you'd never run out of things to do there!'

There are four hotels and a club plus everything from safaris to shopping in between. Importantly for golfers there are two top golf courses to choose from. The Gary Player Golf Course – the signature layout here – was rated by *Golf Digest* as the 99th best course in the world in 2016.

South African great Gary Player designed the course with American Ron Kirby in 1979. They integrated huge bunkers and massive greens into the layout. The walking-only course had a makeover in 2010, removing some bunkers and giving the par-4 9th an island green, according to *Golf Digest*.

As well as having plenty of distance to challenge golfers at 7,162 yards (6,549 metres), you'll face challenges like the nasty par-3 3rd, where you must hit over a pond, but stop the ball on the large bean-shaped green before the deep backside bunkers.

The second golf course to play is the Lost City Golf Course, which was also designed by Player in 1993 and was ranked No. 28 by *Golf Digest SA* in 2016 in Africa. It offers an easier challenge with wider fairways but there are plenty of waste bunkers and water hazards, including one on the 13th hole that has dozens of Nile crocodiles living in it. Best to take a drop away from the edge.

The challenges

Gary Player Course: If you don't keep to the fairways you'll be punished in the rough, some of which grows 1.6–3 inches (4–8 centimetres) long, and giant bunkers. Lost City Course: You'll face waste bunkers and must avoid a lot of water hazards – there are some 92,000 feet squared (about 28,000 metres squared) of water features.

OPPOSITE: Lost City Golf Course from the air.

Type of grasses: Bentgrass greens and Kikuyu grass fairways.

When to play: You can play year-round but it is best to tee off early during summer (December – February) as the temperature can reach 42° Celsius.

Par: Gary Player 72, Lost City 72

Yardage: Gary Player 7,832 yards, 7,162 metres
Lost City 7,309 yards, 6,683 metres

Rating: Gary Player 76, Lost City 74

Best hole: Gary Player Course – the 9th hole is a 596-yard (545-metre) par 5 with an island green to hit onto on approach. Lost City Course – the 197-yard (180-metre), par-3 13th is the signature hole.

The pro says: 'Lost City's Hole 13 is the most beautiful hole ever ... Don't be brave and hit it short into the crocodiles. There are also six deep bunkers waiting for you around the green.' – JC Coetzer

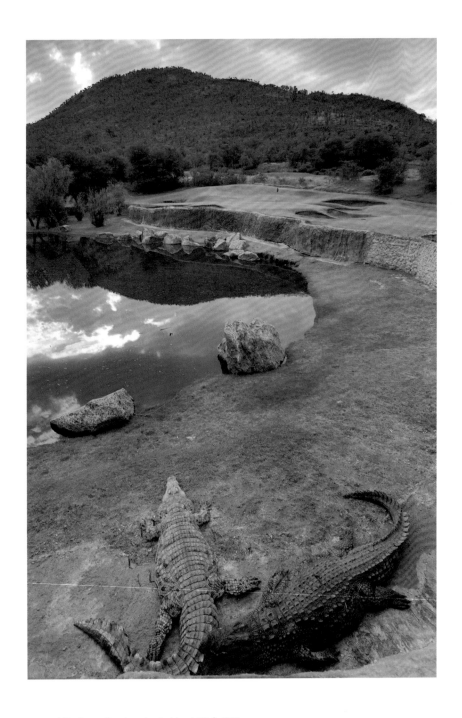

ABOVE: Nile Crocodiles lay short of Lost City's 13th green.

The resort experience

Golf Digest SA editor Stuart McClean rated this as the No. 2 golf resort in Africa. Travellers on every budget can find suitable accommodation here – ranging from the five-star Palace of the Lost City and Cascades Hotel (with three swimming pools), through to the Sun City Hotel (four star), Soho Hotel & Casino, and Cabanas Hotel (three star). The latter is located near the Kamp Kwena Children's Club and Waterworld Lake. Sun City is in the semi-arid North West Province (99 miles or 160 kilometres north-west of Pretoria), so you'll want to be near the pool during summer when the average is over 86° Fahrenheit (30° Celsius).

The Palace, which stands out for its grand architecture, offers a luxurious getaway. From the mosaic artworks and exotic furniture (some use zebra hide), through to the Olympic-sized pool, it is designed to feel like you're staying in an African Palace. Massage treatments can be booked for your room instead of the spa if you are feeling lazy.

Dine and wine

With six eateries to choose from at The Palace alone, it's unlikely you are going to go hungry in Sun City. The pick of them is Plume, a swanky, soulful-looking restaurant which puts African influences on French cuisine (the champagne bar is handy for some bubbly, too). You might also try Crystal Court (international fare), the safari-themed Tusk Bar & Lounge (cocktails), The Grill Room (if you miss your meat), The Palace Gazebo (a private spot for a romantic dinner) and the Palace Pool Deck (wood-fired pizzas, cocktails).

The accommodation

A standard Luxury Twin room (484 square feet, 45 square metres) at the Palace benefits from 24-hour room service, free Wi-Fi and a complimentary English breakfast. You'll enjoy the mountain views from the balcony and some good sleep with the sound-proofing. The height of luxury is the African Suite (2,690 square feet, 250 square metres), with kitchenette, study, dining room, jacuzzis, butler service and your own sauna!

Other activities

You may want to cool down in The Valley of Waves water-park, get lost in the labyrinthine Maze of the Lost City, or get pampered in the Royal Salon. However, there is one must-do adventure here – take a safari through the nearby Pilanesberg National Park where you can see the Big 5 (lion, leopard, elephant, buffalo, and rhinoceros). You can even take a hot air balloon ride over the wild beasts.

Le Chateau Course – Hole No. 10.

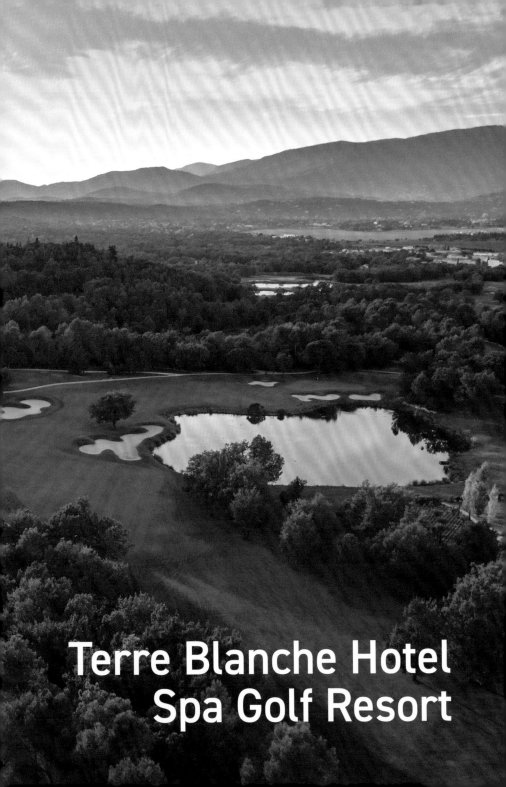

Terre Blanche Hotel
Spa Golf Resort

Tourrettes, The French Riviera, France

Terre Blanche Hotel Spa Golf Resort

Location: 3100 Route de Bagnols en Foret | 83440 Tourrettes Provence, France
Website: en.terre-blanche.com
Phone number: 33 04 94 39 90 00

Set in a beautiful rural setting in Provence, France, some 35 minutes' drive west of Cannes on the French Riviera (or Côte d'Azur), Terre Blanche Spa and Golf Resort is a classic luxury destination with a lot to offer golf travellers. There are two high-quality courses available for hotel guests – Le Château and Le Riou, with the former being the tougher challenge. Designed by the late Welsh professional golfer and architect Dave Thomas, each layout embraced natural features of the land including lakes, valleys, ravines and woods to deliver courses that suit the environment.

Le Château is considerably longer (7,087 yards, 6,480 metres) than Le Riou (6,444 yards, 5,892 metres) and its combination of slick greens and well-positioned water hazards and bunkering make it a championship course of some repute. *Golf World Magazine UK* ranked Le Château No. 13 in its list of *Top 100 Golf Courses in Continental Europe 2016–17*, while Terre Blanche was ranked No. 1 in the *Top 100 Golf Resorts in Continental Europe.*

Le Riou's steep fairways and immaculately kept greens overlook the village of Pays de Fayence. The course, which is open to hotel guests and members, was ranked No. 39 in France by Top100GolfCourses.com in 2017.

Golfers can warm up on the rooftop range, take a lesson (children can go to the Leadbetter Academy) or get their swing fixed using video analysis at the cutting-edge Albatross Golf Performance Centre, a certified European Tour Performance Institute. That is if you can extract yourself from the infinity pool and five-star service at the resort.

The challenges

Le Château course: You'll need a driver off the tee to score well here due to the length, but beware of obstructing trees and bunkers that are positioned in likely landing areas on the undulating fairways – especially on doglegs. There are water hazards on seven holes (2, 4, 5, 8, 10, 11 and 16). The greens are large so it is all about getting your approach near the flag.

Le Riou course: It is shorter but requires more precision off the tee. The club pro

OPPOSITE: Albatross Golf Performance Centre.

recommends using a hybrid or long iron. You'll be hitting over water hazards on Holes 8, 9, 13 and 18.

The resort experience

This five-star resort is constructed like a Provençal village on a hillside, with 115 Suites and Villas (from 646 square feet to 3,229 square feet / 60 square metres to 300 square metres) each with a private terrace and view over the surrounding area. Although pitching itself as a place of natural beauty where you can get away from

Type of grasses: Both courses have fairways of Regenerating Perennial Ryegrass, and greens of Penn A4 Creeping Bentgrass. Ignite grass is used for maintenance.

When to play: Being in the sunny south of France, both courses play year-round.

Par: Le Château 72, Le Riou 72

Yardage: Le Château: 7,087 yards, 6,481 metres
Le Riou: 6,444 yards, 5,893 metres

Slope: Le Riou 146, Le Château 150

Rating: Le Riou 73.4, Le Château 78.1

Best hole: Le Chateau's 11th is the signature hole with a rock creek that cuts across the fairway and two large bunkers guarding the par 5's green. Le Riou's 18th is regarded as its most memorable, with a stream that runs down the right side of the dogleg right and fairway bunkers all the way down the left of the par 5.

The pro says: 'Terre Blanche has to be considered as a whole. The golf courses are enhanced on the golf side by state-of-the-art practice facilities... Then there is the five-star hotel, the spa and restaurants.'
– Jean-Marie Casella, Director of Golf

the hustle and bustle, it is only 45 minutes' drive from Nice International Airport and even closer to Cannes.

Terre Blanche is billed as a resort for couples and families with youngsters or teenagers due to its mix of activities and places to relax. The centrepiece of Terre Blanche is a 1,966-square-foot (600-square-metre) infinity pool that overlooks the resort, the Provence countryside and nearby villages. Next to the pool are private cabanas where you can stretch out and enjoy the same view. The Spa features an indoor pool that opens to a heated outdoor vitality pool and fragrant garden. It also has 14 massage and treatment rooms available.

Taste buds are not forgotten here either. There are four restaurants, offering a variety of culinary experiences (including one with a Michelin star).

Terre Blanche keeps winning awards for its service, including Europe's Best Luxury Golf Resort Spa and France's Luxury Hideway Spa at the 2016 World Luxury Spa Awards as well as France's Leading Resort at the 2013 World Travel Awards.

Dine and wine

The first place to book yourself into is the Michelin-star Le Faventia, which offers refined contemporary French gastronomy. Led by celebrated chef executive Philippe Jourdin, who received two Michelin stars when he joined the resort in 2003, expect fine local wines to compliment dishes such as Bœuf Français De Race (French beef

ABOVE: Resort Infinity Pool; *OPPOSITE:* Indoor Spa.

fillet tournedos with duck foie gras, roasted then smoked with vine cuttings and served with Seillans wine and aged port sauce).

You can also head to Le Gaudina (breakfast or brunch in a cool setting), Le Tousco (salads, pizza and burgers by the pool), Les Caroubiers (gourmet and original dishes at the clubhouse) and Le Pitchoun (a buffet for children up to 12 years old).

The accommodation

The separate white stone and red clay suites and villas make it feel like a village community rather than a hotel. Once inside, you'll notice a mix of contemporary and traditional Provençal décor and light interiors. The creature comforts include heated bathroom tiles, double vanity bathrooms, a lounge and a private terrace. The most luxurious option is the Premier Villa, which also has a separate living room, large terrace, dining area and two bathrooms.

Other activities

An impressive variety of outdoor adventures await in Provence. Explore some of Europe's biggest canyons at Verdon Gorges, tour local vineyards on an electric bicycle, visit the perfumeries of Grasse, or take in the lavender fields on the road to Avignon. Terre Blanche can organize half- or full-day trips to these locations as well as some other great activities. The brave can take a gliding lesson at the aerodrome at Fayence to get a complete view of the area from the air in silence, or take a helicopter tour instead. I'll be spending a day on the Riveria and travelling to St Tropez and Pampelonne Beach by boat.

The Palmer Course – Hole 17, with
Turtle Bay Resort in the background.

Turtle Bay

Oahu, Hawaii, United States

Turtle Bay

Location: 57–091 Kamehameha Highway, Kahuku, O'ahu, Hawaii, United States
Website: www.turtlebayresort.com/Hawaii-Golf
Phone number: 1 866 475 2567

This outstanding resort sits on Oahu's North Shore, not too far from the famous big-wave surf breaks of Banzai Pipeline and Waimea. It features two courses, one designed by Arnold Palmer and Ed Seay and the original George Fazio course. The Palmer course is regarded as the superior design. The first nine holes offer a links-style layout with water hazards and fairways more exposed to the trade winds. The second nine is set in a wooded wetland and the Punaho'olapa Marsh bird sanctuary. The course was ranked 78 in *Golf Digest*'s list of *America's 100 Greatest Public Courses* in 2015–16 and has played host to the Champions Tour and LPGA.

The challenges
A healthy mix of bunkers, both on fairways and around the green, plus water hazards and strategically-placed trees to contend with. The prevailing easterly wind makes the first nine holes harder to contend with. The undulating greens must also be read well.

The resort experience
Turtle Bay is the perfect spot for a romantic getaway or to take the family. It's located on a point overlooking the picturesque bay, and the friendly staff will help you unwind. The resort opened in 1972 with keen golfer Bob Hope as the main act, but it doesn't show its age and regularly ranks as one of the top holiday destinations in Hawaii, taking *Travel Pulse*'s Best Family Hotel / Resort, Hawaii Travvy Award in 2016. The Aloha spirit is alive here.

Dine and wine
There are seven restaurants to choose from, including Pa'akai's fresh seafood (such as the Onaga, a long-tailed red snapper) and the Sunset & Pool Bar, which features a poolside luau with Polynesian dancers.

The accommodation
Luxury rooms and suites can be selected in the main resort building, or you can choose a smaller, more private villa. Many rooms have a great view of the bay. The superb beach cottage I stayed in had one of the biggest bath tubs I've ever seen.

OPPOSITE: Palmer Course.

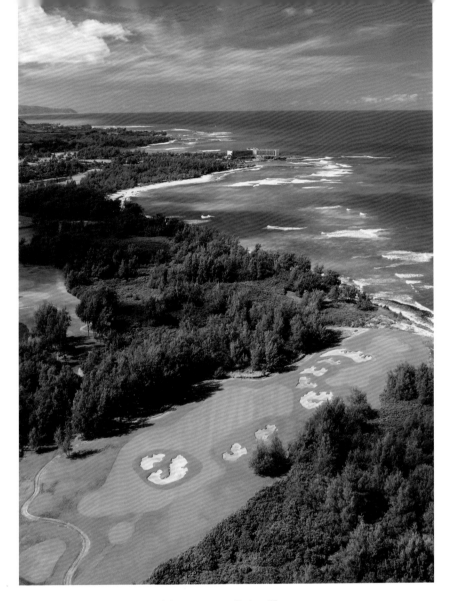

Type of grasses: Lush Paspalum fairways and Sea Island 2000 Paspalum greens – a dense surface suitable for warm, year-round locations.

When to play: Year-round.

Par: 72

Yardage: 7,218 yards, 6,600 metres

Slope: 143

Rating: 75

Best hole: Palmer course. Hole three, named 'Pa Ahamanu' or 'Strong Winds of Kahuku' is one of the best challenges here. A lake straddles the left side of the par 5, a huge sand bunker sits in the middle of the fairway for your approach shot, and a bay must be cleared on the left side as well.

The spa, salon and fitness centre have everything from meditation and aromatherapy to nail care and 'bacial' deep-pore cleansing. There's even spa treatment for kids and teens.

Other activities
Sign up for a two-hour lesson at Hans Hedemann Surf School (hanshedemannsurf. com) and get ready to paddle out on a longboard to the point beside Turtle Bay resort. It's a magnificent experience for beginners and comes with all the bragging rights of surfing Oahu's famous North Shore. But it doesn't stop there – you can enjoy a guided kayaking tour of Kawela Bay, snorkeling with sea turtles, stand-up paddle boarding, horse-riding along ocean-side trails, guided mountain biking, Segway tours and tennis.

ABOVE: Palmer Course. *OPPOSITE ABOVE:* Kayaking at Turtle Bay; *BELOW:* The point break in front of Turtle Bay Resort is great for surfing.

Vidago Palace Hotel

Vidago Palace Hotel

Location: Vidago Park, Apartado 16, 5425-307 Vidago – Portugal
Website: www.vidagopalace.com/en/
Phone number: 351 276 990 900

The Vidago Palace Hotel was built during the reign of Portugal's King Carlos I as a summer retreat next to mineral water springs, but opened for business as a hotel in 1910 after Carlos met his untimely demise and his son, King Manuel II, fled the country under threat. It's located in Northern Portugal, about 1.5 hour's drive from the coastal city of Porto. The resort is about 50 minutes' drive to the Douro Valley region, an area famous for its wines and ports and one recognized for three World Heritage Sites by UNESCO.

But before you try the port you must conquer the golf course, which has two distinct halves. Scottish architect Philip Mackenzie Ross designed the original par-32, nine-hole course on the extensive palace grounds in 1936. It was then renovated, extended and transformed into a championship 18-hole course in 2010 by British design group Cameron Powell.

The front half starts in the beautiful Centennial Park before descending into the Oura Valley for 11 holes. The final three holes return to the top of the Centennial Park with a panoramic view of the surrounding hills and villages. The elevated tees – which have impressive granite retaining walls – and greens both offer great vantage points over the parkland. Vidago's fairways are lined with hundred-year-old trees and the bunkers are strategically placed within sight to test your distance judgment and control.

The original holes offer plenty of challenges. The 180-yard (165-metre) hole 3 is a tricky early test, with a stream running across the front of a green that also has five bunkers flanking it. The green has two tiers and narrows at the back. The 530-yard (485-metre) hole 4 has a stream down the right side of the fairway before crossing it near a green that also has four bunkers sitting in front of it. The challenge continues on the newer back nine, with the 377-yard (345-metre) hole 13 offering a similar test. The Vidago Palace course hosted the Portugal Senior Open in 2014.

The challenges
Some narrower fairways lined by trees, but also plenty of elevation changes as well as smartly-placed bunkers around greens and streams to avoid. The advice here is to play the regulation three shots on par 5s to stay out of trouble.

The resort experience
Vidago Palace has the heritage and grandeur of a castle built for a king, but since it

was completely renovated in 2010 to mark the hotel's centenary, it is now regarded as one of the most luxurious resorts in Europe. Vidago Palace was named the Best Luxury Spa Hotel in the World at the World Luxury Hotel Awards in 2015 and the Best International Spa 2016 at the *Condé Nast Traveller Awards* 2016. Well-travelled European golf writer Jo Maes rates Vidago Palace as one of the top 10 golf resorts he has stayed and played at in the world.

'The hotel combines old but renovated charm with modern design and sumptuous luxury,' Maes said. 'With multiple restaurants and food to match, a spa with water derived from the old thermal baths and tranquility in abundance, Vidago Palace is

Type of grasses: Tees and fairways: a blend of Lollium perenne and Poa pratensis (Kentucky bluegrass). Greens: Agrostis Stolonifera Alpha (Creeping Bentgrass). Rough: Fescue and Poa pratensis.

When to play: Year-round, although frost and sometimes fog can delay the opening of the course during winter months from December to February.

Par: 72

Yardage: 6,938 yards; 6,308 metres

Slope: 73.8

Rating: 141

Best hole: Hole 17 is the signature hole and is regarded as one of the most striking holes in Portugal for its stunning views and dramatic elevation change. Dubbed 'Eagle's Nest,' golfers tee off on the highest point of the course and play to a green that sits on the lowest point. The undulating fairway doglegs to the right on the par 5.

The designer says: 'We have strived to retain the integrity of the original design and to consciously reflect its aesthetics, playability and spirit.' – Cameron Powell *

a place away from it all. Within driving distance of the Douro Valley vineyards and the historic city of Porto, it's an ideal retreat.'

Dine and wine
Some great dining options here. Gourmet restaurant Salão Nobre offers classic Portuguese and signature dishes by Portuguese MasterChef, Rui Paula (with one Michelin Star). You'll also find elegant settings to dine in the Grand Ballroom and Four Seasons Room. Bathed in natural light under a glass skylight, the Winter Garden offers a romantic spot with fresh fruit and pastries for breakfast. The Wine Bar provides great local drops but you can also buy local produce such as cheeses, olive oil and bottled fruit and vegetables. For more informal dining, try the Club House Bar and Restaurant or the Pool Bar.

The accommodation
There are 70 rooms and suites in total, starting at Classic Room and moving through to a more luxurious Suite (with living room/library, Italian furniture, dressing room). Each accommodation features contemporary but elegant décor, bright interiors, designer furniture, views of the park, bathrooms with modern fixtures and creature comforts that would have surprised poor King Carlos I (like the LCD TV and porcelain accessories.)

ABOVE: Vidago Palace Hotel
OPPOSITE ABOVE: Suite; *BELOW:* Salao Noble Restaurant.

Other activities

At the resort, you must try the thermal spa. Vidago Palace was built on an estate with three springs that produce natural carbonated mineral water that became known for its healing properties (it was a favorite with the aristocracy; they still bottle and sell Vidago water). The spa, which was designed by Pritzker Architecture Prize winner Alvaro Siza Vieira on 247 acres (100 hectares) of scented cedar and pine, uses this same water source for a variety of therapeutic treatments, including an ice fountain and vitality pool.

Off site, you must head to the Douro Valley to sample the port wine at vineyards that have been fermenting grapes for 2000 years.

*Source: www.cameronpowell.com/ vidago_palace_golf_course.html

The National Golf Course.

The Westin
Abu Dhabi Golf
Resort and Spa

The Westin Abu Dhabi Golf Resort and Spa

Location: Abu Dhabi Golf Club, Sas Al Nakhl, Abu Dhabi, 126797, United Arab Emirates
Website: marriott.com/en-us/hotels/auhgw-the-westin-abu-dhabi-golf-resort-and-spa/overview
Phone number: +971 2 6169999

Abu Dhabi, the capital the United Arab Emirates, sits on the coast of the Persian Gulf and the edge of the Arabian Desert. It is an arid climate that is not conducive to cultivating lush fairways and greens for golf. But just as the city has seen massive investment and development since 2000, witnessed in buildings such as Etihad Towers, golf courses are being constructed like man-made oases. Architects such as Gary Player (Saadiyat Beach) and Kyle Phillips (Yas Links) have been brought in to develop world-class golf courses. The Abu Dhabi Golf Club – also known as The National – opened in October 2000. Designed by veteran Swiss architect Peter Harradine, it is considered one of the top courses in the United Arab Emirates. The par-72, 7,440 championship course hosts the Abu Dhabi HSBC Championship, a PGA European Tour event that attracts some of the top players in the world each January with a massive purse.

The desert land offered little in the way of natural features and elevation changes to include in the layout, which now has 90 bunkers and seven lakes. The golf course had to be completely manufactured. It was an unusual challenge for Harradine.

'The National was a salt flat, we didn't have a site to work with at all… There were no contours whatsoever – it was completely flat,' Harradine said in an interview with NBC Golf Channel. 'We brought in a lot of sand to raise it and, of course, it's all artificial what you see. The National is artificial. It was great because you could play god a bit.'

The championship layout has large bunkers around the greens (many in the shape of puzzle pieces) and fairways weave between the lakes and palm trees. With a rating of 75.8, this is a tough course.

Harradine was also instrumental in the design of the unusual-looking clubhouse, with a roof in the shape of a falcon that has its wings outstretched and a massive glass front that allows three levels to look out on the golf course.

'It was the first golf course in Abu Dhabi, so obviously it had to be something a bit unusual… we had to create an iconic clubhouse.'

The course is also floodlit and you are invited to play nine holes during the day and nine holes at night like a day-night cricket match.

OPPOSITE: the National's falcon-shaped club house.

When to play: Year-round, although July and August have average temperatures approaching 100° Fahrenheit (or 37.7° Celsius)**.

Par: 72

Yardage: 7,440 yards, 6,803 metres

Slope: 141

Rating: 75.8

Best hole: The par-4 17th will see you hitting over a lake off the tee before the fairway doglegs to the right. There are three fairway bunkers to avoid and another two flanking the front of the green.

The designer says: 'I think its success is that it is not too difficult and it can be played by the normal player. The fairways are wide, there aren't many hazards.' ***
– Peter Harradine

Guests can also play a 3,299-yard (3,017-metre), par-36 nine-hole course that is far easier.

With the luxurious Westin Abu Dhabi Golf Resort and Spa built next to the course and ready to book your tee times, this is one of the top golfing destinations in the Middle East.

The challenges

From the back tees, this is a long course. The layout is generally flat but errant shots can easily find the lakes – water hazards are on 12 holes – or large bunkers.

The resort experience

The Westin Abu Dhabi Golf Resort and Spa is located in the Sas Al Nakhl area, a short drive from the CBD and Abu Dhabi International Airport. The large main building is a light tan brick construction with falcon-shaped roofs. The chic interior is a mix of textured white-brick columns, dark wood panels and marble flooring. There are six restaurants at the property as well as the Heavenly Spa situated in lush gardens. Here, staff offer beauty treatments, such as facials and full-body wraps, and massage therapy for men and women in six treatment rooms. Given how hot it gets in summer, the 7,535-square-foot (700-square-metre) lagoon-shaped main pool will be a welcome retreat. There's also a lap-pool surrounded by palm trees.

I like that checkout is at 12pm.

LEFT: Hotel lobby; *RIGHT:* Lounging Area.

Dine and wine

I'll be booking into Italian at Sacci to try the Risotto di Mare with lobster claws, Atlantic prawns, scallops and baby squid served with the cuttlefish risotto. Elsewhere you can enjoy a buffet at Fairways, pub cuisine at The Retreat sports bar, cocktails and seafood at the plush Lemon & Lime Lounge, vegetarian dishes or burgers at Shades Pool Bar, and fresh coffee at The Lounge. Kids can also get a pass for all-inclusive dining.

Abu Dhabi Golf Club house has some fine dining at The Grille for seafood and steak, lunch and beers at Café 28, and drinks by the club's pool at the Championship Lounge.

The accommodation

There are 172 rooms, including 19 suites with modern interiors and contemporary décor. Starting at the Deluxe Room (484 square feet, 45 square metres), which has the option of a king-size bed or two twins to sleep three people, floor-to-ceiling-glass doors onto a balcony overlooking the golf course, plus a work desk. The Presidential Suite (5,113 square feet, 475 square metres) has two master bedrooms, a spa, living room, work area, kitchen, and three terraces with views. Some rooms, such as this, come with breakfast included. Free Wi-Fi is provided throughout.

Other activities

Guests at the Westin receive complimentary access to the Saadiyat Beach Club, a facility that sits next to the turquoise waters of the Persian Gulf, approximately 30 minutes' drive away. It features a 6,997-square-foot (650-square-metre) outdoor pool that you can roll into off the cabanas that are right next to it. There's also a spa in the club and restaurants, too. The 5.6-mile (9-kilometre) stretch of beach that Saadiyat sits on is a protected habitat for Hawksbill turtles.

In the city, I'll be heading up to the Observation Deck at 300, which can be found on the 74th floor of Tower 2 of the Etihad Towers. You get a spectacular view of Abu Dhabi from 984 feet (300 metres).

Abu Dhabi has some fun family attractions, too, including the nearby Ferrari World, which has rides such as the Formula Rosa rollercoaster that reaches a speed of 149 mph (240 km/h) in five seconds. The Yas Waterworld has dozens of rides and slides, including a 771-foot (235-metre) Tornado waterslide. Then the Wadi Adventure park has a man-made surf pool, white-water rafting, and kayaking, too.

Back at the resort, the WestinWorkout Gear Lending Program provides clean workout gear, including joggers, if you didn't pack your own. The resort will also provide trail maps for local 3- and 5-mile (5- and 8-km) routes.

*Source: oobgolf.com/courses/scorecard.php?id=314881

**Source: holiday-weather.com/abu_dhabi/averages/

***Source: www.golfchannel.com/media-golfing-world-meet-course-designer-peter-harradine/

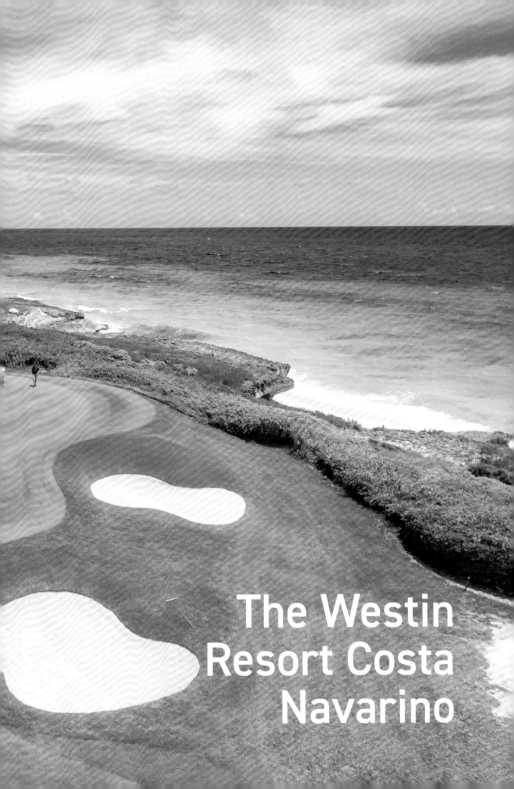

The Westin
Resort Costa
Navarino

Plyos, Greece

The Westin Resort Costa Navarino

Location: Navarino Dunes, Messinia, Costa Navarino, 24001, Greece
Website: costanavarinogolf.com ; westincostanavarino.com
Phone number: 30 272 309 5000

This resort in the southwest Peloponnese – a peninsula in Southern Greece that stretches into the Mediterranean and Ionian Seas – has a moral story to it, according to European golf writer Jo Maes, who recommended this golfing destination.

'Captain Vassilis Constanakopoulos, who came from humble origins, founded what was to become one of Greece's biggest cargo shipping companies,' Maes said. 'His ultimate vision was to return to his home region with an investment plan that would put it on the world map as a quality destination and at the same time, bring much needed economic development to an area often forgotten.'

Captain Constanakopoulos achieved his dream with Costa Navarino Resort, which features two five-star luxury hotels, luxury residences, spa centres and a holiday destination with a great range of facilities. There are leisure and sporting activities aplenty here, but golfers will be drawn to two high-quality championship courses – the Dunes Course and the Bay Course.

The Bay Course was designed by Robert Trent Jones II in 2011 and is laid out alongside Navarino Bay, the site of a decisive naval battle in October 1827 that saw Allied forces (Russian, English and French) defeat an Ottoman armada (Tunisian and Egyptian), a result that helped secure Greece's independence. The par-71 course demands strategic play and accurate hitting as you move along the seashore. There are some tremendous views of the coastline with lush fairways set against the pale-blue Ionian Sea and rocky mountains in the backdrop. Get the camera ready for the 'The Grove', 'Seaside' and 'Canyon' holes. The Bay Course was named 'Greece's Best Golf Course 2015' at the World Golf Awards.

The Dunes Course was designed by German great Bernhard Langer with European Golf Design and opened in 2010. The links-style layout works its way next to the resort complex, moving past citrus and olive groves and a small meandering river towards the sea. The fairways are open, but watch out for the pot bunkers and undulating greens. Again there are some special ocean views to enjoy, especially on the par-4 2nd hole. The Dunes was ranked the No.1 course in Greece by Top100GolfCourses.com in 2017.

OPPOSITE: The Dunes Course.

The challenges

Keep your ball on the fairway on both courses or risk a high score. The Dunes is the harder challenge here, however, with its deep pot-holed bunkers, undulating fairways and large, sloping greens. The wind can increase the difficulty on both links-style courses.

Type of grasses: Bentgrass for the greens and Bermuda grass on the fairways for both courses.

When to play: Both courses close in November and open in February.

Par: Dunes Course 71, Bay Course 71

Slope / Rating / Yardage: Dunes Course 110 / 73 / 6,581 yards, 6,018 metres Bay Course 136 / 71 / 6,140 yards, 5,614 metres

Best hole: On the Dunes Course, the par-4 hole 2 plays downhill with the ocean serving as a shimmering backdrop. There are three fairway bunkers, two on the left and one on the right to contend with. On the Bay Course, hole 1 is a driveable par 4 at 318 yards (291 metres) but you must carry a lake. Hole 4 (391 yards, 358

metres), is a stunner, too, with the town of Pylos in the backdrop.

The pro says: 'The Dunes Course is a tough test of your golf, especially the front nine. It has a good balance of tough and easier holes to keep you interested always and add balance to your round. The Bay Course stands as a unique course for its amazing views and the mix of sea and Olive Trees. There are no other courses like The Bay Course. Even if you play badly you still walk off with a smile. All in all, it is a shorter, tighter golf course with breathtaking sea views from at least 12/13 of the holes. The Bay's smaller greens with subtle undulations give you a chance to make a good score.'
– Yiannis Tsioukanis, British PGA Qualified Professional and Golf Manager

The resort experience

Costa Navarino was named 'European Golf Resort of the Year – 2017' by the International Association of Golf Tour Operators (IAGTO). There are two luxury hotel options for visitors to the Greek holiday destination – The Romanos (www.romanoscostanavarino.com) with 321 rooms and villas, and the Westin – both of which have appeared on *Condé Nast Traveller* gold lists.

'All products and most staff are sourced locally which has revived this part of Greece and has made Costa Navarino into one of the most iconic resorts in Europe,' said European golf writer Jo Maes. 'There are two more courses planned: Navarino Hills and Navarino Blue.'

The Westin has 445 rooms and suites that have been created in the tradition of old mansions, with most looking out on the sea and golf courses. Many of the ground-floor apartments feature infinity pools, a good spot to watch the sunset.

The Westin is a golf hotel the whole family will enjoy. While adults might be drawn to the Anazoe Spa, which has treatments based on the teachings of legendary Greek physician Hippocrates, the factor that makes this resort stand out are the activities for the kids. There's an aquapark with waterslides and pools, as well as a recreation park with indoor basketball, badminton, table tennis and volleyball. Children's clubs Cocoon (four months to three years) will keep the littlees busy with painting and clay, Sandcastle (four years to 12 years) will challenge them to arts and crafts, and the Youth Club will get teens on a team playing everything from football to volleyball.

ABOVE: The Lagoon Pool. OPPOSITE: View from accommodation.

Dine and wine

The Westin aims to delight your palate by using organic ingredients and local fare from the Messinia countryside. The variety of foods on offer is impressive – with a total of 12 restaurants and eateries. Mories has a Greek breakfast buffet; Flame has signature meat cuts served on wooden platters; Da Luigi is for lovers of Italian; Taverna has homemade-style Greek dishes; Barbouni will serve your afternoon meal by the beach; Inbi has fusion Japanese; Armyra serves fresh seafood and Nargile looks after Lebanese food. Plus the Diner is an American-style diner, Souvlakerie has you traditional souvlaki, Kafenio & Deli will sort your coffee, and then Kayak Ice Cream Boatique is perfect for a scoop of dessert.

The accommodation

You'll find 11 types of rooms and suites to choose from with modern interiors and décor and tiled flooring. A Deluxe Room (420 feet squared, 39 metres squared) can sleep two adults and two children on a sofa bed and two singles, and comes with a private balcony or patio and separate shower and tub. At the other end of the scale, a two-bedroom Premium Infinity Suite (753 feet squared, 70 metres squared) can sleep up to six guests. It has an infinity pool, enlarged terrace and outdoor dining area.

Other activities

As mentioned, the kids' activities, which include indoor sports facilities, are outstanding. But there are plenty of fun outings for the adults, too. The Westinworkout Gym has a 69-foot (21-metre) pool, two steam rooms, two saunas, a whirlpool and relaxation room plus yoga, Pilates and aqua-gym sessions. Navarino has professional guides for hiking to historical sites, climbing at Proti Island or mountain biking local trails. The racquet academy features nine sports, including tennis and squash. Navarino Sea Under Water can take you to some great scuba diving sites in the turquoise water, including to a World War II wreck and Seal's Cave where Caretta Caretta turtles can sometimes be spotted. Speedsters can also get their thrills at the Navarino Speed Experience Park in 270cc racing karts. Water-skiing, yachting, kitesurfing, kayaking, yachting (half-day to two-day cruises)… the list keeps going.

Barnbougle Dunes/Lost Farm, Tasmania, Australia.

THE EXPERTS

Thank-you to the following experts who helped me select these golf resorts:

Dave Finn (Canada):
Dave Finn is a freelance golf travel writer and photographer who has played over 750 golf courses in 25 countries. He is a three-time award recipient from the Golf Journalists Association of Canada and the Travel Media Association of Canada, and the Canadian correspondent for the Top100GolfCourses.com.

Robert Fagan (US):
One of the most respected golf writers in the world, Bob has played more than 3,000 courses. A former professional who has won at the state, collegiate, and professional levels within the US, he also served as a PGA Section Executive Director. The author of more than 1,400 articles/books, Bob Fagan has produced the DVD/audio book *Golf's Higher Plane* about the emotional side of the game, and written golf course guides for California, Hawaii, and America.

Masa Nishijima (Japan):
Design consultant and author of *Analysis of a Golf Course* and co-author of *The Confidential Guide to Golf Courses – Volumes 1, 2 and 3*. Masa has played more than 2,300 courses in 56 countries.

Stuart McLean (South Africa):
Stuart McLean is the Editor of *Golf Digest SA* and author of *South African Golf Courses: A Portrait of the Best and South Africa's Greatest Golf Destinations*.

Ulrich Mayring (Germany):
Ulrich Mayring has reviewed more than 250 golf courses across Europe, contributed to *The World Atlas of Golf*, and is the German correspondent for Top100Golf-Courses.com.

Larry Berle (US):
Larry Berle is the author of *A Golfer's Dream*, about one man's journey to play *Golf Digest's* Top 100 Courses.

Nick Cutler (Australia):
Nick Cutler is the managing Director of CustomMade Media Australia, publisher of *Australian Golf Digest*.

Jo Maes (Ireland):
Jo Maes is the President of the European Golf & Travel Media Association and Managing Director of par4our golf advisers. Jo has played more than 325 of the best courses and visited over 100 golf resorts around the world.

Hwa Young Nam (South Korea):
Hwa young Nam is the former Editor-in-Chief of *Golf Digest Korea*, author of *Golf Tips from Tour Pros*, Editor of *World's 100 Best Golf Courses You Can Play* and Chief Editor of *Herald Sports*.

Ernie Els (South Africa):
Ernie Els, a professional golfer, former world No. 1 with four major wins and renowned course architect.

Fergal O'Leary (Ireland):
Fergal O'Leary completed the *Golf Magazine* US Top 100 at age 28 and completed the *Golf Magazine* World Top 100 at age 32 in 2015. Fergal is the youngest person in history to complete the US 100 and the World 100, and is the only Irishman to complete either feat. He is an active panelist with *Golf Magazine*, reviewing courses around the world, and also serves as the US correspondent on Top100Golf-Courses.com.

Anita Draycott (Canada):
Anita Draycott is a Toronto-based golf writer, editor and photographer with more than 25 years experience. Anita has played more than 1,000 courses on six continents and is columnist for Travelindustrytoday.com's *Fairways to Heaven*.

Michael Clayton (Australia):
Michael Clayton is a former professional on the PGA European Tour and PGA Tour of Australasia, golf broadcaster, golf writer and acclaimed course designer.

Tom Doak (US):
Tom Doak is the owner of Renaissance Golf Design, architect of courses including Barnbougle Dunes and Cape Kidnappers, and co-author and editor of *The Confidential Guide to Golf Courses*, now being republished as a five-volume set.

Darius Oliver (Australia):
Darius Oliver is a golf course designer, author and publisher of the *Planet Golf* series and co-author of *The Confidential Guide to Golf Courses – Volumes 1, 2 and 3*. Darius has visited more than 1,500 golf courses worldwide.

A NOTE OF GRATITUDE

This book is dedicated to my father Paul Fallon, a champion, my mother Coralie, and our families. I want to express my gratitude to the golf writers, experts, professionals, course architects, and tourist bureau personnel who helped me select the golf resorts in this book. In particular, I'd like to thank Dave Finn (Canada), Robert Fagan (US), Masa Nishijima (Japan), Stuart McLean (South Africa), Ulrich Mayring (Germany), Larry Berle (US), Jo Maes (Ireland), Hwa Young Nam (South Korea), Ernie Els (South Africa), Fergal O'Leary (Ireland), Anita Draycott (Canada), Nick Cutler (Australia), Michael Clayton (Australia), Tom Doak (US) and Darius Oliver (Australia) for their input. Many of these fine and well-travelled golf writers and professionals are also the authors of acclaimed golf books and much better golfers than I am!

I would also like to thank the great people from the golf resorts and courses for their assistance and for hosting me, especially the resort photographers for the stunning images that have been contributed to this book. The guidance and encouragement of New Holland's Alan Whiticker as well as travel editor Helen Anderson and authors Susan Wyndham and Phillipa McGuinness, and inspiration from authors and friends Jon Casimir and Helen Greenwood were invaluable to this project. Thank you.

A special thanks to my beautiful wife Rebecca and our gorgeous children, Joey, Julia and Annie, as well as my parents, Paul and Coralie Fallon, for their love and constant support of my endeavors. Also, thank you to my Australian family and friends for your encouragement, and my American family, led by Jim and Rose Granich, for your support.

With admiration and my sincere thanks,

Daniel Fallon

OPPOSITE: Casa De Campo, La Romana, Dominican Republic.

Fairmont St Andrews,
Fife, Scotland.

IMAGE CREDITS:

Pages 20–27: Photography by Kohler.
Pages 50–51: The Bluffs Ho Tram Hole No. 1, photo by Tom Eubank.
Page 211: Blackstone Course – Hole No. 15, photo by Tom Breazale.
Pages 258-9-159: © Rosewood Tucker's Point.

ABOUT THE AUTHOR

Daniel Fallon is a journalist, editor, travel writer, copywriter, composer, saxophonist, handballer and avid golfer. During his 17-year term at The Sydney Morning Herald, travel assignments took him to some of the best golf courses and resorts in the United States, Australia, and New Zealand. Daniel has more than 20 years' media experience and has worked for leading companies including Fairfax Media and ACP (now Bauer Media) as a section editor, magazine editor and online editor. As Digital Night Editor of The Sydney Morning Herald he covered breaking world and entertainment news online while based in the United States between 2013–16. Daniel is a senior content producer at the BBC and manages a Sydney bureau for the broadcaster. Most importantly, he is the loving husband of Rebecca and father of Joey, Julia and Annie Fallon.

First published as Golf Resorts around the World in 2017 by New Holland Publishers

Published in 2023 by New Holland Publishers Sydney

Level 1, 178 Fox Valley Road, Wahroonga, NSW 2076, Australia

newhollandpublishers.com

A record of this book is held at the National Library of Australia.

ISBN 9781760794699

Managing Director: Fiona Schultz
Publisher: Alan Whiticker
Editor: Pete Malicki
Designer: Andrew Davies
Production Director: Arlene Gippert
Printed in China

10 9 8 7 6 5 4 3 2 1